Project
Management

Other titles in the Briefcase Books series include:

To learn more about titles in the Briefcase Books series go to
www.briefcasebooks.com

You'll find the tables of contents, downloadable sample chapters, information about the authors, discussion guides for using these books in training programs, and more.

Project Management

Gary R. Heerkens, PMP

McGraw-Hill

New York Chicago San Francisco Lisbon Madrid
Mexico City Milan New Delhi San Juan
Seoul Singapore Sydney Toronto

McGraw-Hill

A Division of The **McGraw·Hill** Companies

1 2 3 4 5 6 7 8 9 0 AGM/AGM 0 9 8 7 6 5 4 3 2 1

ISBN 0-07-137952-5

This is a CWL Publishing Enterprises Book, *developed and produced for
McGraw-Hill by* CWL Publishing Enterprises, *John A. Woods, President. For
more information, contact CWL Publishing Enterprises, 3010 Irvington Way,
Madison, WI 53713-3414, www.cwlpub.com. Robert Magnan served as editor.
For McGraw-Hill, the sponsoring editor is Catherine Dassopoulos, and the
publisher is Jeffrey Krames.*

Printed and bound by Quebecor World Martinsburg.

This publication is designed to provide accurate and authoritative information in regard to the subject matter covered. It is sold with the understanding
that neither the author nor the publisher is engaged in rendering legal,
accounting, or other professional service. If legal advice or other expert
assistance is required, the services of a competent professional person
should be sought.
    —*From a Declaration of Principles jointly adopted by a Committee
    of the American Bar Association and a Committee of Publishers*

McGraw-Hill books are available at special quantity discounts to use as pre-
miums and sale promotions, or for use in corporate training programs. For
more information, please write to the Director of Special Sales, McGraw-Hill,
2 Penn Plaza, New York, NY 10121. Or contact your local bookstore.

 This book is printed on recycled, acid-free paper containing a minimum of 50% recycled de-inked fiber.

Contents

Preface

This book chronicles the exploits of Brad—a fictional character who's been thrust into the wonderful world of project management. Just like many project management professionals I've met in my many years in the field, he was drawn into the battle reluctantly, but he emerged wanting more.

And as you will soon discover, project management is actually a curious combination of art and science. The artistry refers to the leadership part of the role, or the *people component*. The science—which we will explore with Brad—consists of the tools and techniques that form the underpinnings of the entire project management process. But instead of simply providing information on project management tools and their proper use, this book will explore the *principles* behind their use. This marriage of tools and the principles behind them yields a powerful, plain-language guide that not only explains *how* to do things, but *why* they need to be done.

The book presents a *realistic* view of project management— a very difficult, yet rewarding profession. The role of project manager is a particularly challenging job. Actually, many practicing project managers consider overcoming challenges to be the essence of their job. So this book explores project management from the standpoint of challenges. The very first chapter, in fact, explores the question of whether you should even take on the role at all! Don't let me scare you though. This book—if you stick with it—will provide all of the tools and techniques you'll need to overcome just about any problem related to the science of project management.

The first three chapters lay out everything you need to know about projects, project management, and the role of project manager. Establishing a foundation of understanding in these areas will provide the context you need to better understand the world you (and Brad) are about to enter.

Brad's first big challenge unfolds in Chapter 4, as he tries to figure out exactly what he's supposed to do! All too often, project managers are given half-baked ideas that they must convert into viable, feasible, money-making ventures. This isn't easy. Chapter 4 will show you how to define your project so that everyone understands what it will accomplish, and agrees that it is a worthwhile undertaking.

Building and maintaining an effective team is always challenging. Chapter 5 offers a host of practical tips for getting the right people, providing the right amount of direction, and ensuring that people will be standing in line to work on your next project.

Few would argue against the understanding that planning is the heart of project management. Planning is so important, in fact, that I've devoted two chapters to this subject. Project managers are under tremendous pressure to "just get on with the work." Consequently, project planning is sometimes short-changed. Chapter 6 helps you understand the function and purpose of planning, and offers insights on the challenges you can expect to face as you strive to prepare your project plan. Once this groundwork of understanding is laid, Chapter 7 shows you the nuts and bolts of planning, step by step.

One of the biggest single challenges all project managers face is risk and uncertainty. By their very nature, projects are one-time events. This means that you don't really know what to expect or how things are going to turn out. Chapter 8 will show you how to address that challenge so as to, if not eliminate risk, manage it effectively.

Chapter 9 describes how you can stay in control while the project work is being done, even though there are many different people doing many different things. The key to tackling this challenge, as you will see, is information. And plenty of it.

Chapter 10 shows you how to mange the environment that surrounds your project. Just like Brad, you will discover that there are a myriad of people and things trying to tug your project in different directions. In this chapter, you'll learn how to manage your project interfaces in an effective manner.

Effective communication and proper documentation are threads that bind the project together. The biggest challenge you'll face in this area, however, is likely to come from within. Many people do not communicate as effectively as they would like, and many try to avoid documentation. If either of these situations describes you, be sure to read Chapter 11. You'll find many tips and techniques that will enhance your understanding of communication and documentation from the project manager's perspective.

Eventually, your project will come to an end. Brad discovered that this part of the project is surprisingly challenging. Confusion and chaos are not unlikely in the waning days of the project. Chapter 12 shows you how you can cut through the chaos and drive your project to a successful conclusion.

Brad's adventure in managing Project Apex was an incredible learning experience for him, as I trust this book will be for you. Obviously, you can't learn everything there is to know about project management in a single book. That's OK. Most of what you will eventually learn about project management will come from your on-the-job experience. The intent of this book is to provide practical tips and techniques that will open the door for your self-development, and allow you to get the most from your experiences.

Being an excellent project manager requires years of practice. For many, however, getting started is the toughest part. This book, I am certain, will get you off to an excellent start.

Special Features

The idea behind the books in the Briefcase Series is to give you practical information written in a friendly person-to-person style. The chapters are short, deal with tactical issues, and include lots of examples. They also feature numerous boxed sidebars

designed to give you different types of specific information.
Here's a description of the boxes you'll find in this book.

 These boxes do just what they say: give you tips and
tactics for being smart in the way in which you plan and
execute the management of your project.

 These boxes provide warnings for where things could
go wrong during every phase of the project management process.

 Here you'll find the kind of how-to hints the pros use to
make your project go as smoothly as possible.

 Every activity has its special jargon and terms. These
boxes provide definitions of these concepts.

 Look for these boxes for examples of principles and
practices described in the text.

 Here you'll find specific procedures and techniques
you can use to manage your project more effectively.

 How can you be sure you won't make a mistake some-
time as you manage your project? You can't. But if you
see a box like this, it will give you practical advice on
how to minimize the possibility.

Acknowledgments

The ideas and learnings expressed in this book were shaped
from countless discussions with project management profes-

sionals and many other associates willing to share their experiences, insights, and opinions. Unfortunately, I cannot list all of the people who helped me learn how to manage projects, or all of my friends and colleagues in the Project Management Institute who have helped to broaden my knowledge. But I do appreciate them nonetheless.

And I would be remiss if I did not acknowledge the contribution of the many students who have attended my seminars, and were willing to discuss the problems and issues confronting them—they have provided some of the most valuable insights of all.

I would also like to acknowledge the contribution of Don Lindsay, a visionary leader who shaped my thinking and professional behavior more than any other organizational manager throughout my long career.

For helping me improve the product, I'd like to thank Frank Saladis, PMP, for his willingness to review my manuscript and offer his insights and suggestions. I'd also like to thank Mary Russo for her help in transcribing my marginally successful attempt at trying to make this part of the "books on tape" series!

I'd also like to thank John Woods from CWL Publishing Enterprises for recruiting me to write this book and for his perseverance and latitude. He kept telling me that I'd be pleased and proud when I was done. He was right. Bob Magnan, also of CWL, was responsible for much of the final editing, and I appreciate the polish he put on this work.

Finally, I wish to thank my wife, Sandra, and sons, Gregory and Russell, for their support, patience, and understanding through some difficult periods—and throughout the countless hours of solitude they allowed me to impose on myself, and the countless hours of silence I imposed upon them.

About the Author

Gary R. Heerkens, PMP, PE is a consultant, trainer, lecturer, and author in the field of project management. He is the president of Management Solutions Group, a Rochester, New York based company that specializes in providing project management educational solutions and organizational development support.

Prior to founding Management Solutions Group, Gary managed a wide variety of project types and sizes for 20 years at a *Fortune* 100 company. He designed and taught several project management training programs, helped develop project process methodology, and acted as an internal project management consultant across the company.

In addition to teaching and consulting, Gary is a contributing editor to *Successful Project Management*, a nationally circulated newsletter, and a member of the review committee for the Project Management Institute's (PMI) *A Framework for Project Management* seminar.

He is a frequent speaker at international project management conferences. He has been certified as a Project Management Professional (PMP), and as a licensed Professional Engineer in New York State. He served as the president of the Rochester Chapter of PMI from 1998-2001. He holds BSME and MBA degrees from the Rochester Institute of Technology. You can reach Gary via his company's site on the Internet, www.4msginc.com.

Congratulations ... You're the Project Manager!

Brad picks up the phone before the second ring. It's his boss, Susan. "Brad, I'd like you to stop by my office right after lunch today."

Brad is not really sure why the boss is calling him into her office, which makes for a long lunch hour. He knows he's been doing a good job lately. As a matter of fact, he knows that he's probably the most technically capable person in the group.

Brad's mind begins to race.... Maybe it's an award? Could it be a promotion?

"No, wait," he says to himself in a frenzy of self-doubt. "Maybe I did something I wasn't supposed to? Or maybe I didn't do something I should have?"

Countless positive and negative scenarios run through Brad's overworked mind until one o'clock finally rolls around and he cautiously enters Susan's office.

"Brad, I've got some great news for you," Susan begins. "Since it's so closely related to what we do here, Project Apex has been assigned to our group." Brad smiles without knowing why.

Susan continues, "You're one of the best engineers I have." Brad's smile widens in anticipation. And then—without warning—Susan utters those fateful words. "Congratulations, Brad, I'm assigning you as the project manager for Project Apex."

Great news? Did she say *great* news? "What do I know about managing projects?" Brad thinks to himself.

As Brad begins to leave Susan's office, she delivers the knockout punch. "By the way, Brad," Susan says with a curious inflection in her voice, "I think you should be aware ... management is *really* going to be watching closely. There's an awful lot resting on the success of your project."

As Brad slips out of Susan's office, the same two words keep ringing in his ears—"*your project.*"

The Accidental Project Manager

The story above is not an isolated incident. Every day, engineers, salespeople, technicians, and countless others are thrust into the role of project manager. They're very good at what they do. In fact, they're typically the most technically knowledgeable engineers or the most successful salespeople. Now they're about to become project managers.

Actually it's probably appropriate to refer to them by their more popular (however informal) name—*accidental project managers*. An accidental project manager is a person who is placed into the role by organizational necessity and chance, rather than by design or through choice of career path.

> **Key Term**
>
> **Project** "A temporary endeavor undertaken to create a unique product or service," according to the Project Management Institute.
>
> **Project manager** The person ultimately responsible for the success or failure of a project.
>
> **Accidental project manager** A person who is placed into the role of project manager by organizational necessity and chance, rather than by design or through choice of career path.

**The Pros and Cons of Becoming
a Project Manager**

Pros:
- It can often be a steppingstone to promotion.
- It provides a strong sense of accomplishment.
- There's considerable variety: no two days are alike.
- There's significant freedom of choice.
- It affords the opportunity to effect change across the organization.

Cons:
- It requires significant tolerance for politics.
- It requires significant tolerance for ambiguity and uncertainty.
- There's a lot of responsibility, but little or no authority.
- You may feel "disconnected" from your technical discipline.
- You may be perceived by some as not having "a real job."

If you're an accidental project manager, one of the first things you should do is pause to consider whether or not you're cut out to be a project manager and try to determine whether it's what you really want to do. Why? Because if you do a reasonably good job leading your first project, chances are you'll be asked again. And again. And again. In other words, if you're finding yourself in the same position as Brad, you might be embarking upon a new career. You'd be wise to consider some of the pros and cons before saying yes to that career move.

The information, tools, and techniques presented in this book will move you well along in understanding the mechanics of managing projects. But it's important that you enter this new world with your eyes wide open. With that thought in mind, let's take a closer look at what you might expect to experience as a project manager.

What Can You Expect to Encounter "Out There"?

Although you won't often see it addressed in project management reference books, the reality is that *mental preparedness* may prove to be just as critical to your ultimate success as a project manager as your knowledge base or skill set. And gaining a sound understanding of what's involved in this new role is a critical step toward being mentally prepared. So let's explore those pros and cons in a bit more detail by describing the life of a typical project manager—assuming there is such a thing.

However Brad may feel about taking on his first project, the truth is that life as a project manager can be extremely rewarding. You'll find it to be different from most any other thing you've ever done. It's complex, varied, and interesting. If done well, it can lead to a very strong sense of accomplishment. These are among the aspects that project managers identify as the main draws to the job.

At the same time, however, being a project manager will test you in ways you may not be able to imagine now. You will become a focal point in the organization. Everyone will look to you for the answers, but you must be careful not to try to provide all the answers; after all, that's why you have a team.

And speaking of the team, one of the biggest shifts in behavior (and thinking) you'll encounter will be the need to rely upon others to get things done. In most cases, that's your team. You'll quickly discover that there's far too much for you to do alone, yet delegation will prove to be a challenge for you. Empowering others, and then trusting them to follow through, may be a bit unsettling. You'll find yourself uncomfortable with the idea that others are doing things for which you will be held responsible.

You'll have lots of responsibility, but you'll be missing the authority often perceived as being required to discharge that responsibility. You'll have to get things done through the people on your team without having any *direct* control over them. Among

---

Smart Managing

Hang in There, Baby!

If you can get experienced project managers to let their guard down for a few moments, they'll probably admit that their first few projects didn't go very well—and that's the sugar-coated version. So be prepared for a rough start as you begin to manage projects. But if you hang in there, you'll find yourself moving up the learning curve rapidly. In the world of project management, experience is a particularly powerful and effective teacher.

your most valued tools will be the ability to persuade and influence, as you seek to form a group of diverse personalities into a unified team with commonalty of purpose.

Unfortunately, not everyone on your team will be as knowledgeable and skilled as you would like. Nonetheless, you've got to get the job done using whatever resources have been provided. Project management lore is full of tales of project managers who were able to take "the hand that was dealt" and turn it into project success. For you to succeed, you'll have to rely on your ability to coach, mentor, and motivate in order to get the level of performance you need from those assigned to work on your project.

What will you have to know as a project manager? Well, you'll have to know a little bit about just about everything. You'll have to learn to pay attention to the details, but not get wrapped up in them. You'll have to make countless decisions with insufficient information and despite conflicting signals. You'll have to condition yourself to seek *acceptable* solutions, rather than *perfect* ones. You'll have to blend technical expertise with a keen sense of human nature. You'll have to handle administrative matters.

And while you're busy doing your own thing, you'll have to cultivate and maintain a smooth working relationship with *many* other people, both inside and outside your organization. Unfortunately, as you seek to carry out the objectives of the project, it's unlikely that everyone you encounter will be an ally. Organizational politics and reality dictate that not everyone will like project management or project managers (that's you!). Many people will admire your role, respect your position, and appreciate your involvement; others will not. You will need to figure out who's who—real fast.

But at the end of the project, you'll be able to look back and feel a deep sense of pride that comes with producing a successful outcome and creating positive change. Project leadership requires the use of many different skill sets. It involves tasks of limitless variety. You must live by a curious combination of

Smart Managing

Uncovering the Potholes on the Road to Success

Be proactive in determining who's likely to work with you and who's likely to work against you by arranging informal chats with key individuals within your organization. Initiate a casual discussion about the discipline of project management. In many cases, it won't take very much time to figure out whether you can expect your relationship with that individual to be relatively smooth or to be rocky.

process compliance and individual judgment, of gut feelings and data, of people and things. The challenge is enormous.

So if you feel *mentally* prepared to accept this challenge, you're well on your way to becoming a successful project manager. The only thing left is to learn how to do it the right way.

Throughout this book, we'll tell you and show you how to do project management the right way. And although we'll focus primarily upon the process, we'll never lose sight of the importance of the interpersonal aspects as well as the environmental aspects—the people and things that surround your project. Together, the process and the people form the art and science of project management.

About the Art and Science of Project Management

Project management has two major aspects:

- the art—leading the people on the project
- the science—defining and coordinating the work to be done

The art of project management relates to the fact that projects are really about people getting things done. Project management requires a keen knowledge of human behavior and the ability to skillfully apply appropriate interpersonal skills.

The second aspect—and the focus of this book—involves the knowledge, understanding, and skillful application of a prescribed *project management process.* This process is intended to guide project managers and project teams in effectively performing key process steps, such as identifying the true need, defining the project objective, creating an execution schedule, and maintaining control throughout the entire project. The basic premise of the process is the development of a set of graphic tools, documents, and techniques, all aimed at facilitating project success. Among the graphic tools and documents are the Requirements Document, the Work Breakdown Structure, and the Network Diagram (all covered in chapters to come). Among the many techniques we'll cover will be calculating Net Present Value, preparing a comprehensive proposal, and conducting a Make vs. Buy Analysis.

About This Book

As we focus on the tools and techniques of project management throughout this book, we'll be making a few key assumptions intended to represent the most common conditions for practicing project managers today. First, we'll assume that you are the person leading the project—irrespective of your position within the organizational hierarchy. Second, we'll assume that you are managing projects within a *matrix environment*. This means that the project requires the efforts of individuals from a number of functional departments, such as Marketing, Engineering, Human Resources, Operations, etc. Finally, we'll assume that you do not have direct control over these people; in other words, you are *not* their immediate supervisor.

However, even if you're not a practicing project manager, if you're a manager of project managers or an executive, this book will be of great value to you. It will provide you with a wealth of knowledge and insight relative to the life of a project manager. This knowledge and insight will greatly help you develop a meaningful support structure for the project managers *and* project teams within your organization. Few would deny that project managers stand a much better chance of effectively applying the tools and techniques covered in this book and therefore succeeding with their projects when they operate within a supportive organizational environment. And if you're a supervisory manager or organizational executive, you play a primary role in ensuring that a supportive environment is provided for project managers—like Brad.

Project Manager's Checklist for Chapter 1

❑ Project management is both an art and a science. The art is strongly tied to the interpersonal aspects—the business of leading people. The science (which this book will focus on) includes understanding of processes, tools and techniques.

❑ All project managers are expected to be very well versed in the science of project management. You cannot survive without being knowledgeable in this area.

❑ If you're an accidental project manager (put into the role rather than choosing it voluntarily), you'd better pause to think about whether you're cut out to be a project manager before getting too involved. Although it can be personally satisfying, it's a tough job that requires a thick skin. If you do a good job, you'll probably be asked to lead many more projects, so you'd better be OK with the role, or your life will not be much fun

❑ Generally speaking, the project manager's job is not intellectually challenging, but it is complex and broad. It requires a large variety of different skills—many of which will be new to you.

About Projects and Project Management

Upon returning to his desk, Brad contemplates what lies ahead. Although a bit frightened, he likes the idea of taking on a new challenge.

"The visibility should help my career along," he says to himself with a wry smile, "... as long as Project Apex turns out OK, that is," the smile turning gradually into a slight grimace. As he polishes off the turkey sandwich he was too nervous to finish before meeting with Susan, he decides to accept the assignment—though he's not sure he *really* has a choice!

Before tackling Project Apex, Brad realizes that he'd better do a quick study on project management—starting with the basics of what a project is and how project management is supposed to be done. He wants to be in the best possible position to make Project Apex a resounding success. Let's give him some help by examining project management from three perspectives:

1. the process context
2. the interpersonal and behavioral context
3. the organizational context.

Project Management: The Process Context

Problems, needs, and opportunities continually arise in every organization. Problems like low operational efficiency, needs like additional office space, and opportunities like penetrating a new product market are just a few of a nearly endless number of situations that management must address in the process of operating an organization or company. These problems, needs, and opportunities give rise to the identification of solutions. Executing those solutions entails a change for the organization. Projects are generally established to carry out this change and there's always someone responsible for the successful completion of each project. As the project manager, you are the primary change agent, and your guide for carrying out the change is the *project management process.*

What Is a Project?

Several definitions exist for "project." We used a simple one in Chapter 1: "A temporary endeavor undertaken to achieve a particular aim." Whichever specific definition you choose, nearly every project you manage will have many of the same characteristics. Let's examine some of the most important ones.

At the most basic level, a project is actually *the response to a need, the solution to a problem.* Further, it's a solution that promises a benefit—typically a financial benefit. The fundamental purpose for most projects is to either *make money* or *save money.* That's why projects should be financially justifiable, as we'll see in Chapter 4.

By definition, a project is *temporary in nature*; that means that it has a specific start and finish. A project consists of a *well-defined collection of small jobs* (tasks) and ordinarily *culminates in the creation of an end product or products* (deliverables). There will be *a preferred sequence of execution* for the project's tasks (the schedule).

A project is a *unique, one-time undertaking;* it will never again be done exactly the same way, by the same people, and within the same environment. This is a noteworthy point, as it suggests that you will rarely have the benefit of a wealth of historical information when you start your project. You'll have to launch your project with limited information or, worse yet, misinformation.

There will always be some *uncertainty* associated with your project. This uncertainty represents *risk*—an ever-present threat to your ability to make definitive plans and predict outcomes with high levels of confidence. All of your projects *consume resources*—resources in the form of time, money, materials, and labor. One of your primary missions is to serve as the overall steward of these resources—to apply them as sparingly and as effectively as possible.

So, there's a general definition or explanation. Here are some examples of projects: introducing a new product to the marketplace, building and installing a piece of equipment, and running a political campaign. In contrast, the following activities are not projects: operating a manufacturing facility, supervising a work group, and running a retail business. These activities are ongoing.

What Is Project Management?

The Project Management Institute defines project management as "… the application of knowledge, skills, tools and techniques to project activities to meet project requirements" (*A Guide to the Project Management Body of Knowledge,* 2000 Edition, Newtown Square, PA: Project Management Institute, 2000, p. 6). Although this definition may sound pretty straightforward, you will find that the skillful application of those skills, tools, and techniques will come only after you've had a significant amount of education and on-the-job experience.

The project management process calls for the creation of a small organizational structure (the project team), which is often a microcosm of the larger organization. Once the team has produced the desired outcome, the process then calls for the decommissioning of that small organizational structure.

The Project Life Cycle: The View from 50,000 Feet

Projects typically have identifiable phases and each phase has a unique set of challenges for the project manager. If we view the project process from the highest level, four basic project phases can be identified.

During the first of these four phases, the *Initiation Phase*, the need is identified. An appropriate response to the need is determined and described. (This is actually where the project begins.) The major deliverables and the participating work groups are identified. The team begins to take shape. Issues of feasibility (*can* we do the project?) and justification (*should* we do the project?) are addressed.

Next is the *Planning Phase*, where the project solution is further developed in as much detail as possible. Intermediate work products (interim deliverables) are identified, along with the strategy for producing them. Formulating this strategy begins with the definition of the required elements of work (tasks) and the optimum sequence for executing them (the schedule). Estimates are made regarding the amount of time and money needed to perform the work and when the work is to be done. The question of feasibility and justification surfaces again, as formal approval to proceed with the project is ordinarily sought before continuing.

During the third phase, the *Execution Phase*, the prescribed work is performed under the watchful eye of the project manager. Progress is continuously monitored and appropriate adjustments are made and recorded as variances from the original plan. Throughout this phase, the project team remains focused on meeting the objectives developed and agreed upon at the outset of the project.

During the final phase, or the *Close-Out Phase*, the emphasis is on verifying that the project has satisfied or will satisfy the original need. Ideally, the project culminates with a smooth transition from *deliverable creation* (the project) to *deliverable utilization* (the post-project life cycle). The project customer accepts and uses the deliverables. Throughout this phase, project resources (the members of the project team) are gradually re-deployed and the project finally shuts down. However, although the project team and the project manager typically stop participating at this point, they can benefit greatly from understanding and appreciating what goes on *after* the project, as we will soon see.

The Project Management Process: Step by Step

Now that we've overviewed the process, let's circle back and break it down into steps. I recommend an approach that follows the four-phase model described above, but provides for additional detail in the areas of *requirements gathering, project definition, risk management,* and *stakeholder management.* The result is the eight-step process, which we'll use as the basis of study in this book. The eight steps are briefly summarized below:

Step 1. Identify and frame the problem or opportunity. In this phase, the fundamental need is identified. The need is then quantified with respect to factors such as its size, shape, and extent. This leads to the creation of a *Requirements Document,* which articulates the need in as much detail as possible.

The true need must be completely understood before attempting to define the best solution. A significant number of project failures can be attributed to the phenomenon of *solution-jumping.* In simple terms, this occurs when you try to provide an answer without understanding the question. This is a real possibility whenever the requirements are not fully defined, and impulse—rather than a rational process—is used to determine the project solution.

> **Solution-jumping** The tendency of people to talk about what to do before analyzing the situation adequately, trying to develop a solution before thoroughly understanding the problem.
>
> *Key Term*

Step 2. Identify and define the best project solution. In Step 2, early determinations should be made regarding which work groups should be involved. A team should be formed to assist in this and all subsequent process steps. This step begins by identifying all reasonable alternatives. The team may use brainstorming or similar creativity techniques to help identify alterna-

Amy's Need

Dave walked briskly over to Bill's cubicle. "Bill, I just got a call from Amy. She's got a problem and needs our help. I'd like you to go over there right away and get the details. Figure out what she needs and take care of her."

Bill was pleased to be assigned to one of his organization's most valued clients. By the next afternoon, he was sitting in Amy's office, carefully reviewing the documents she'd prepared.

"Bill, we need the capability of screening all of our incoming components *before* they come into the assembly line," said Amy. "You're free to do this any way you'd like; just make sure that they fall within these guidelines." She handed Bill some design documents and a list entitled *Incoming Material Screening Requirements*.

Bill was happy that Amy had given him free rein in determining the solution to her problem. He studied the project requirements and formed a project team. Then, he and his team developed and installed the hardware and software necessary to check all incoming components for compliance with the screening requirements. It was truly a thing of beauty. Bill was proud of the job he and his team had done.

Less than a week later, Dave called Bill into his office. "Bill, Amy just called me," he said. "They're still having the same problem as before— *too many rejects coming off the end of their assembly line*. What happened?"

Suddenly Bill realized what had happened. He had just discovered Amy's true need—the hard way.

tive solutions. Using criteria previously agreed upon, the team then singles out the "best" solution. *This is the actual project.* The team prepares project definition documents, which consist of a comprehensive narrative description of the preferred execution approach, the criteria for project completion, and the definition of project success. In many organizations, this step concludes with a formal proposal to management and formal approval or authorization to proceed is granted. If the project is not approved, it may be terminated.

Step 3. Identify task and resource requirements.

Once the project solution is identified, we're ready to move to the next phase, which is to identify the task and the resource requirements. This is also referred to as *scope management*. In this step, the team identifies all of the work to be done (the tasks). Consideration should be given to the preferred methods for doing the work and how much of the work will be done using internal resources. Preliminary resource commitments should be secured for all work.

Step 4. Prepare the control schedule and resource allocation plan. Creating the project schedule consists of several steps. First, a network or logic diagram is prepared to display the *optimum sequencing* of the tasks. Next, the length of time required to complete each task (its *duration*) is estimated.

By combining information on the preferred sequence of tasks, the estimated task durations, and an assumed project start date, the team can place tasks in "real time," much like scheduling appointments on a calendar. This reveals the total project duration and the expected project completion date. The final part of this step consists of creating a logic-based, time-scaled bar chart that will be used during the project execution to track progress.

Step 5. Estimate project costs and prepare a project budget. In this step, the project manager coordinates the preparation of a cost estimate for the project. A variety of methods may be used to estimate cost, depending upon the level of detail that exists at that time. The overall project cost is allocated to individual elements of the project, thus creating a budget for each major work element. This budget is used to monitor and control cost expenditures during project execution.

Step 6. Analyze risk and establish stakeholder relationships.
Once the project team has identified the work, prepared the schedule, and estimated the costs, the three fundamental components of the planning process are complete. This is an excellent time to identify and try to deal with anything that might pose a threat to the successful completion of the project. This is called *risk management.* In risk management, "high-threat" potential problems are identified. Action is taken on each high-threat potential problem, either to reduce the probability that the problem will occur or to reduce the impact on the project if it does occur. Though treated as a discrete step, risk analysis should be a continuous process: you should be ever vigilant for threats to your project's success.

> **Key Term**
>
> **Project stakeholder** Anyone who has a vested interest in your project. This group ordinarily includes those who stand to gain or lose through the success or failure of your project, those who participate in the execution of your project, those who supply resources to your project, and those who are affected by the outcome or outputs of your project.

This is also a good time to identify all the project stakeholders and establish or solidify relationships that will be maintained throughout the life of the project.

Step 7. Maintain control and communicate as needed during execution. You'll spend most of your time in this step. During project execution, people are carrying out the tasks and progress information is being reported through regular team meetings. The team uses this information to maintain control over the direction of the project and takes corrective action as needed.

The first course of action should always be to bring the project back "on course," to return to the original plan. If that cannot happen, the team should record variations from the original plan and record and publish modifications to the plan. Throughout this step, organizational managers and other key stakeholders should be kept informed of project status according to an agreed-upon frequency and format. The plan should be updated and published on a regular basis. Status reports should always emphasize the anticipated end point in terms of cost, schedule, and quality of deliverables.

Step 8. Manage to an orderly close-out. This step is often characterized by the development of a *punch list.* A punch list is a relatively small list of tasks that the project team needs to complete in order to close out the project. The project manager must keep team members focused at this critical time. Unfortunately, far too often the attention of the team begins to drift because the project is shutting down. If this step of the process is not managed in an orderly fashion, the end can have a tendency to drag on. This can have a devastating effect on customer satisfaction.

Finally, the team should conduct *lessons learned studies,* to examine what went well and what didn't. Through this type of analysis, the wisdom of experience is transferred back to the project organization, which will help future project teams.

> **Punch list** A relatively small list of tasks that the project team needs to complete in order to close out the project.

What Happens What "After the Project" Is More Important than the Project

Are you shocked? Insulted? Don't be. This doesn't mean that what you do during the project has little value. It simply points out that your approach to nearly everything throughout the eight steps of the project management process should be heavily influenced by your knowledge of what will happen *after* you've produced the project deliverables.

As mentioned above, the deliverables that your project produces will be accepted and used by a customer, client, or user.

Accordingly, your knowledge of how, why, when, and where your project's deliverables will be used should form the basis for making decisions throughout the entire life of the project. This is called *managing the project with a full life cycle perspective.* This perspective recognizes the fact that many of the decisions you make *during* the project will have far-reaching and profound effects on the efficiency, productivity, utilization, and profitability of the project deliverables *after* the project has been completed.

Project Management: The Interpersonal and Behavioral Context

Although this book focuses primarily on process, a full and fair treatment of project management would not be complete without some discussion of interpersonal and behavioral aspects of project management. You will find that the interpersonal and behavioral aspects of project life are crucial to the success of a project. In fact, studies often point to interpersonal and behavioral problems as a root causes for project failure. As mentioned previously, the art of project management is about dealing with people and about getting work done through other people. So let's take a closer look at the phenomenon of project leadership.

The Phenomenon of Project Leadership

In his book entitled *Project Management as if People Mattered* (Bala Cynwyd, PA: Primavera Press, 1989), Dr. Robert J. Graham makes several critical distinctions about the phenomenon of project leadership, which I'd like to pass along. Together, these statements do an excellent job of characterizing the interpersonal and behavioral side of project management.

Leading a project is not the same as leading a department. A project by definition is unique; it has never been done before. As a result, the end product and the process for producing it are never fully specified in advance. Therefore, *the project leader lives in an environment of constant uncertainty.*

The project leader coordinates the efforts of a team of people who may not be accustomed to working with one another.

They will normally have a wide variety of skills, backgrounds, biases, work habits, values, and ethics. *The project leader must work with this diverse group of people so that they coalesce into an effective working team.*

Project teams normally cut across organizational boundaries and include people from several departments or groups. Project success will require the cooperation of all of these people. To gain this cooperation is often a challenge. *The project leader must be skilled in obtaining cooperation from other people over whom he or she does not have direct control.*

In today's organizational environment, good human relations skills are vital to success in project work. The task is difficult for project leaders who are leading a team formed of diverse personalities, operating in a temporary and uncertain environment, and trying to obtain cooperation from people over which they have no direct control.

This issue of direct control is worth repeating, because it's so important. One of the most difficult aspects of your position as a project manager relates to the simple reality that in most organizations it's unlikely that project managers will have direct control or formal authority over the people on the project team. This is fundamentally different from leading a department, where the manager ordinarily exercises formal control and a hierarchical relationship between supervisor and subordinate is recognized as the norm. Project leaders, lacking formal authority, must rely on influence and persuasion to gain cooperation. Their skills in this area are integral to their role as project managers.

Motivating Your Team: Giving 'Em What They Need

Beyond possessing the ability to influence the people on your team to get the desired performance, you must also learn how to motivate them, to keep them energized toward meeting goals. This is a somewhat controversial topic.

Can you truly motivate the individuals on your team? Most experts think not, primarily because motivation is viewed as an internal function. You should recognize, however, that you can

Practical Tips for Creating a Motivational Climate

Tip # 1: Convey the attitude that people and their work are valued

- Take time to explain how each member's function contributes to project goals.
- Take time at team meetings to highlight how various members contribute to positive results.
- Heighten the exposure of low visibility or less appreciated responsibilities.

Tip #2: Convey Confidence in People's Knowledge, Ability, and Work Ethic

- Avoid double-checking and micromanagement as much as possible.
- Assign goals that represent a stretch for the individual, then let him or her determine how best to achieve those goals.
- Provide freedom, decision-making power, and authority in a way that conveys trust.

Tip #3: Recognize Good Performance

- Clarify in advance what represents a high standard of performance.
- Communicate achievements of your team to management in a visible and positive way.
- Openly recognize *attempts* to go beyond what's expected.

Tip #4: Lead by Example

- Don't ask others to do things that you would not be willing to do yourself.
- Intercede on behalf of members of your team when warranted.
- Continuously maintain the highest levels of honesty and integrity at all times.

create a climate, environment, or situation where motivation can occur within an individual. Motivation is all about recognizing a need that exists within an individual and finding a way to satisfy that need. This is a key point in understanding how to develop a high-performing team.

Managing Diverse Objectives and Perspectives

Most project teams are made up of people from several departments. As a project manager, one of your jobs is to form the team into a unified, single-minded unit with a focused project objective.

Occasionally, however, individual team members may have their own objectives (some call it a hidden agenda), based upon their personal situation, technical discipline, or feelings of allegiance toward their work group. When team members have multiple personal objectives, it can undercut team cohesion and weaken the team's dedication to the project. If you allow individuals too much freedom to pursue their own objectives, it can be counterproductive to the objectives of the project. As your team comes together, you should be attentive to any personal objectives. For example, someone from the marketing department may focus solely upon optimization of product reliability, usefulness to the end user, or customer appeal. A representative of the human resources department may be driven solely by quality of work life issues or workforce morale. These are noble causes, but they must be considered in the context of the larger picture, together with all other factors. Even deeper personal agendas—such as ambition with intent for personal gain at all costs—could create challenging situations for you as the project manager. You must learn to recognize and discourage all kinds of *personal* objectives and be able to focus the entire team on the overall *project* objectives.

Project managers may also have to manage diverse objectives from outside their project teams. Many project managers must work effectively with groups *outside* their organization, such as suppliers, subcontractors, and partners. Members of these groups will often have very parochial perspectives. Getting them to rally behind your project's objectives instead of their own can be quite challenging at times.

Finally, in today's global environment, managing diverse objectives may apply to issues of culture, politics, and customs. People often consider working on teams to be an opportunity to promote their own interests, beliefs, opinions, causes, and so forth. Again, you should value diversity among your team members, but not allow it to distract from your project.

Project Management: The Organizational Context

Most project managers work in organizations. And organizations—large or small—are often complex. Life as a project manager in a complex organization offers many challenges. The
people on your project team will come from different functional
work groups, which creates various leadership challenges for
you. Your organization's management is likely to have an opinion on the value of project management methods. You need to
clearly understand that perspective and what it means to you.
And overall, your entire organization is currently operating at
some level of project management excellence—or maturity.

These and other aspects of organizational life serve as the
backdrop as you seek to discharge your responsibilities as project manager. How well you understand and adapt to these
aspects is what determines your *political savvy*—a key component of your functional competency. Let's explore these organizational issues in a bit more detail.

Overcoming the "Silo Mentality"

Most organizations consist of many functional departments.
Normally there's a representative from each affected department on the project team. Each individual team member's perspective—or frame of reference—will tend to align with his or
her discipline or work group. This is the *silo mentality*.

The challenge for you is to redirect team members' frame of
reference from a *functional* orientation to a *project* orientation.
Encourage them to think in terms of what's best for the

Silo mentality When people in an organization tend to
think first of the needs, interests, and goals of their individual departments, before the needs, interests, and goals of the
organization as a whole. Also known as *silo thinking*, the term derives
from diagrams of multi-disciplined organizations, which ordinarily display functional departments in a vertical orientation. Team members
who think exclusively in terms of their own work group are said to be
thinking in "functional silos" (vertically), rather than in terms of what's
best across the entire project (horizontal thinking).

project. Coach them, for example, to refrain from making decisions that optimize their part of the project until they've verified that someone else's part will not be adversely affected. (Obviously, this is easier said than done!)

One of the best ways to get team members to work across function lines is by using project management discipline and applying project management techniques. Project management is the glue that binds your "temporary organization" together. You must tirelessly promote the idea that every team member must focus on what's best for the project.

How Does Your Management View Projects?

Projects are often viewed as being fundamentally rooted in technology. This is because most projects are technical. Unfortunately, this orientation toward technology has obscured the true purpose of projects. The truth is that projects are all about business—not technology. The fundamental objective for a project is to achieve a business result, such as improving effectiveness, increasing sales, or making operations more efficient. No matter what that underlying cause, the ultimate purpose of a project is very simple: to make money or to save money. That's management's expectation as well—or at least it should be. Most organizations are paying closer attention to the return on their project dollar.

This has process implications, such as ensuring that you place a strong emphasis on preparing the *business case* for your project during the early stage—a business case that clearly shows anticipated expenditures vs. savings, cost-benefit ratios, and the anticipated business impact on the organization. These business-related project expectations have implications for you as a project manager. In addition to being technically knowledgeable, you should know about business methods, business strategy, and business skills. You should adopt an entrepreneurial spirit in the way you execute your projects. In short, the expectation is that you should manage your project as if you were a businessperson starting up a small enterprise.

What Is Your Organization's "Level of Maturity"?

Project management maturity is a concept that has received greater attention over the past few years. The project management maturity of your organization has a tremendous effect upon the way that project management discipline is carried out within the organization and tends to define what your life as a project manager will be like. There are several views on how best to measure and characterize an organization's project management maturity, but most identify anywhere from three to five levels of maturity. Whatever process is used to describe maturity, the metrics usually attempt to gauge these parameters (in no particular order):

- The extent to which project process documentation has been developed and distributed and is understood throughout the organization
- The ability of project teams to predict outcomes with reasonable accuracy
- The efficiency with which projects are executed
- The perceived success rate of projects
- The organization's ability to learn from its experiences
- The extent of continuous improvement in project execution over time

The combination of your organization's project management maturity and your management's opinion of the value, purpose, and function of project management will often dictate the boundaries of your authority and responsibility as a project manager.

More Dynamics of Managing Projects in Organizations

Those who manage projects in organizations typically must deal with two fundamental problems—cross-functional departments overlaid on a hierarchical authority structure. Functional hierarchies have all sorts of rules that specify, for example, who should make a decision, who should direct the efforts of others, and how people should communicate. Project managers who chronically violate these rules may be subject to organizational sanctions.

There's typically a formal communication process that prescribes how "official" information is to be transferred between departments only through their heads. Thus coordination between departments requires that information and data move up and down the organization. Savvy project managers appreciate that this mode of operating may slow down the process considerably, so they may use informal communication channels whenever possible.

Similarly, there exists within many organizations an informal organization, an informal network of personal contacts and relationships among people in the organization that lies outside the formal structure. It includes friendships and the grapevine, among others. This informal structure does considerable coordination work. For example, the marketing people may contact their friends in design engineering to sort out some low-level technical problems that their customers are experiencing.

When people fail to resolve problems by working within the formal structure, they tend to use the informal structure. For example, a project manager might go beyond his or her authority to approve an expenditure, hoping that the necessary paperwork will be sorted out later. If projects in a functional hierarchy are managed almost entirely through the informal organization, it suggests a need to modify the formal structure so that it's more in line with project management methodology.

The nature of your organization's structure will greatly determine how you work as a project leader. In a *purely functional organization*, decision making and authority will be very strongly oriented toward individual departments or individual functions within the organization. This can make your life tough. At the other end of this continuum exists the *purely projectized organization,* where project managers have tremendous influence, authority, and decision-making power. These are typically organizations whose core business is executing projects, such as large consulting firms. Most organizations are somewhere between these extremes. In these *matrix organizations,* the decision making and the authority are shared between project managers and functional management. As a project manager, you need to understand where your organization resides along this continuum and use this as a basis for determining your limits of authority and participation in the decision-making processes.

Defining Project Success

The definition of project success is obviously critical. After all, that's how you'll be judged as a project manager. Unfortunately, there are almost as many definitions of project success as there are project management professionals. To add to the confusion, every organization has its own view of what matters in project outcomes.

So, instead of trying to focus on one definition, I'd like to offer a *framework of thought* on success. I've found it valuable in the many discussions I've had over the years.

If you consider the various ways that projects could be deemed successful, you come to realize that project success exists on four levels, each with a unique perspective and set of metrics. And despite the specific values used to quantify success or failure, the principle remains constant. Following are the four levels of success that I use:

Level I—Meeting Project Targets

Did the project meet the original targets of cost, schedule, quality, and functionality? Although it's certainly admirable to beat these targets, my concept of success is tied to whether the project manager did what was expected. In other words, maximum success is zero variance between project targets and results. There are at least two reasons why I embrace this interpretation. First, it supports the organization's need for certainty. Second, I believe that project managers who chronically beat targets are suspect, at best.

Level II—Project Efficiency

How well was the project managed? This is a metric for the *process*. If the project meets its targets, but the customer groups, project team, or others were adversely affected by the project experience, the project will probably not be perceived as successful. Project efficiency can be evaluated through the use of criteria such as the following:

> ### Back Up if You Have to
>
> When you're assigned to manage a project, one of your first steps should be to uncover the true need. If you don't, you can't be certain that your project will satisfy that need. Unfortunately, taking time to determine the true need may be viewed by some as "backtracking." But the alternative is to risk being perceived as unsuccessful. So back up if you aren't absolutely sure you understand the true need.

- The degree of disruption to the client's operation
- How effectively resources were applied
- The amount of growth and development of project team members
- How effectively conflict was managed
- The cost of the project management function

Level III—Customer or User Utility

To what extent did the project fulfill its mission of solving a problem, exploiting an opportunity, or otherwise satisfying a need? Earlier in this chapter, Bill was caught in the situation where he managed a project effort that did not solve the client's problem. If, like Bill, you do not satisfy the true need, the project may be perceived as a failure.

Here are some questions to help assess Level III success:

- Was the original problem actually solved?
- Was there a verifiable increase in sales, income, or profit?
- Did we save as much money as expected?
- Is the customer actually using the product as intended?

Level IV—Organizational Improvement

Did the organization learn from the project? Is that knowledge going to improve the chances that future projects will succeed at each of the three levels described above? High-performing organizations will learn from their failures—and their successes—and use that knowledge to improve their success rate in over time. This level assumes a long-term perspective and measures organizational learning and a resultant increase in project successes. The primary tools for organizational improvement are the maintenance of accurate historical records and the widespread use of lessons learned.

Project Manager's Checklist for Chapter 2

❑ Projects possess several key characteristics. They are temporary and unique. They consist of several tasks that have a preferred sequence. They consume resources and result in end products called deliverables. They ordinarily involve high levels of risk and uncertainty.

❑ These and other characteristics make projects different from day-to-day work; projects therefore call for the application of special management techniques.

❑ Projects are carried out in four major stages: *initiation*, where the project is defined and launched, *planning*, where the solution is detailed and the work required to carry it out is identified and scheduled, *execution*, where the work is done and monitored, and *close-out*, where the project is brought to successful closure.

❑ You should manage your project with a full life cycle perspective. This means understanding how the deliverables of your project will be used after the project is handed over to the customer, and using that knowledge to influence the decisions you make during the project.

❑ Most project managers work in complex organizations, where people who work on the team may come from sev-

eral different work groups. This can create unique management challenges for you, as you strive to get everyone
focused on doing what's best for the project.

❏ Project success can be evaluated on four different "levels":
(1) Were the cost, schedule, and deliverable performance
targets met? (2) Was the project managed in an efficient
manner (3) Is the customer happy and have the desired
business results been achieved? and (4) Did organizational learning take place that will lead to better projects in the
future?

The Role of the Project Manager

A s I mentioned in Chapter 1, the project manager's job is extremely diverse—at least you're supposed to make it that way. In fact, the single, most useful piece of advice I'll offer you is "Think like a generalist." This means avoiding the natural tendency to devote too much of your attention to those aspects of the project that are familiar and comfortable. This is just one of the many challenges you can expect to face as you assume the role of project manager. Let's take a closer look at your role by examining it from three angles:

- the responsibilities you'll have
- the challenges you're likely to face
- the skills you'll need to be successful

Your Responsibilities as Project Manager

Your responsibilities fall into four broad areas:

- the project
- your organization

- your team
- yourself

Each area of responsibility has a slightly different focus, adding to the diversity of the role.

The most obvious responsibility is the one to the *project*. You're expected to meet the cost, schedule, functionality, and quality targets. You must run the project efficiently. You must act as an arbiter of the differing objectives that will inevitably exist within and across the team, as discussed in Chapter 2.

You also have a responsibility to your *organization*. The project you're managing is expected to provide a tangible return to your organization. The extent to which you'll be held responsible for guaranteeing this return will be discussed in Chapter 4.

Also, as a project manager, you're viewed as an "agent" of your organization and its management. You're expected to adhere to the policies of the organization, act within the limits of your authority, and generally make decisions that are in the best interests of the organization. That last expectation may be challenging at times, as decisions that benefit your organization may not be best for the project.

Yet another responsibility you have to your organization relates to information flow. This includes honest estimating, timely reporting of status, and accurate forecasting. *Proactively* keeping organizational management informed of project status and forecasts—*good or bad*—is one of your more important responsibilities as a project manager, maybe even critical to your survival. The key word here is *proactively*. If any member of management gets hit by any surprises, if it's revealed that someone is lacking some critical information that he or he should have known, it can be devastating for that person. And if it's because you failed to inform him or her, it can be devastating for you as well.

Keeping your organizational management proactively informed also includes providing them *appropriate* opportunities to intercede as needed in guiding the course of your project. This is yet another aspect of the responsibility you have to your organization.

The responsibilities you have to *your team* will vary from project to project and team to team. They include ensuring that the team is properly informed throughout the project, providing constructive feedback when warranted, and giving positive, fair, and appropriate recognition for performance. These responsibilities are not easy. One of your biggest challenges will be striking an appropriate balance among the needs of the individual team members, the needs of your team as a unit, and the needs of your project. Superior project managers will further accept the informal responsibility for providing growth and development opportunities for individual team members whenever possible.

Your final responsibility is to *yourself.* Though not often discussed in project management textbooks, this responsibility is vital—particularly if you view project management as your chosen profession. The odds are that your organization still does not have well-developed career paths and career development programs geared specifically to project management as a discipline. If you're fortunate enough to have this support, congratulations! If not, then the responsibility for your personal growth and development falls largely upon you. Later in this chapter, we'll explore the role of introspection and self-awareness in this process.

Common Challenges You Can Expect to Face

As mentioned previously, you can expect to face a number of challenges as you take on the responsibility of managing projects in your organization. Whatever the specifics of your particular situation, however, many of the challenges you'll face are faced by most project managers. Let's review a few of these common challenges.

The Responsibility vs. Authority Trap

Firmly embedded in project management folklore is this one: the responsibility you've been given is not commensurate with the authority (or formal power) you believe you need to accomplish the mission. The size of the gap between responsibility and authority will partially depend upon the structure of your organization (as we discussed in Chapter 2). If you're in a purely functional organization—and in many cases, a matrix organization—you should not expect to be granted very much formal authority. The gap between responsibility and authority will be quite wide. To compensate for your perceived lack of formal authority, you'll have to rely upon expert power (respect you can garner through superior knowledge or capability) or referent power (often accessed by practicing an excellent leadership style). You'll also need to rely heavily upon your ability to influence and persuade.

Imposition of Unrealistic Targets

Sound project management practice suggests that project goals (cost, schedule, quality, and functionality) should be determined through a systematic process of understanding customer needs, identifying the best solution, and formal planning. Throughout this process, realistic assumptions about resource availability, quality of materials, and work process (just to name a few factors) should be used. This approach yields a credible estimation of what is reasonably achievable. If this estimation does not meet *business goals*, then a systematic risk-vs.-return process should be pursued until it can be verified whether or not the targets can be met within a given level of elevated risk. *That's the process that should be followed.*

Unfortunately, we live in a real world. Targets are far too often based on desire or a vague sense of what should be achievable, rather than driven by calculated business needs. In even more unfortunate circumstances, targets are developed before it's even known what the project entails! In either case, the result is that impatience—rather than a rational

> **Reverse Scheduling**
>
> **CAUTION!**
>
> If you've been assigned to a project with an imposed end date, avoid the temptation to develop your schedule by starting with the finish date and working your way backward to the current date. This will create a false sense of what is achievable and mask the true level of risk involved in meeting that date. Refer to Chapter 8, Dealing with Risk and Uncertainty for more on this topic.

process—drives the selection of the targets. From that point on, a desperate struggle begins, as the team tries to force the project to fit within the boundaries that have been drawn.

This practice puts project managers in a very difficult position, as it often sets them up for certain failure and severely undermines the planning process. Unfortunately, this phenomenon seems to have reached epidemic proportion: it's one of the biggest complaints of practicing project managers today.

Perpetual Emphasis on Function

If you're managing a project in a functionally oriented organization, one of the more difficult challenges that you'll face is getting team members to overcome their inherent tendency to think and act in terms of optimizing their own discipline, technical field, or department. It's important to recognize that this phenomenon is fueled by three powerful influences. First, by definition, projects are temporary, but functions live on. In other words, a person often considers his or her work group to be *home;* the project is just a passing state of existence. Second, unless contemplating a formal career change to project management, a person considers his or her discipline or area of expertise as the *work focus.* This means that her or she will likely be committed to ensuring the well-being of that area. This strong loyalty could, for example, give rise to counterproductive situations, such as team members using *your* project funds to advance *their* discipline—perhaps in excess of what customer requirements dictate. Finally, there's the power of the paycheck. Simply stated, most people tend to pledge allegiance to the source of their paycheck. For most people in most organizations, that's their work group or functional department, not you.

The Dual Responsibility Trap

Most project managers I encounter are asked to wear two hats. They must perform their job duties while acting as the project manager. (Brad is in that position, working as senior technical lead and managing Project Apex.) This situation may present additional challenges for you.

At the center of this dilemma is the issue of allegiance. Imagine for a moment that you're facing a critical decision. Unfortunately, what's best for the project will negatively impact your work group but what benefits your work group will hurt your project. What's the right decision? What do you do? If you make the decision that benefits your work group, you risk being viewed as a poor project manager. If you choose the course of action that benefits the project, you may incur the wrath of your peers and/or departmental management. It's a tough spot—and you can almost bank on being in it, possibly often.

A more fundamental problem of the dual responsibility trap is figuring out how to divide your time and attention between the two roles. How much should you allocate to each? How long can you try to satisfy both before you realize you're working most nights and weekends?

Finally, a third issue often surfaces in the form of the *two boss syndrome*. The project manager reports to his or her functional supervisor and to the person who manages the project management function in the organization. Again, this is a difficult situation for most project managers.

The Fundamental Conflict of Certainty and Uncertainty

Many misunderstandings and disconnects between project managers and organizational management can be traced to the fundamental conflict between the certainty that management requires to properly run the business and the inherent uncertainty of project work. Cost and schedule estimating provides us with an excellent example.

Suppose you're just beginning a project. It's likely that you have limited information on this project and there's a significant degree of uncertainty. In a situation such as this, project management practice suggests that *you would be well advised to use ranges of values when providing estimates* on cost and schedule. The size of your range would reflect a level of accuracy consistent with the extent of your knowledge and the amount of uncertainty. In our example, it would be perfectly appropriate for you to estimate that the cost of your project will be somewhere in the range of $400,000 to $550,000.

Education Is a Lifelong Process

Smart Managing If you're like most project managers I know, you can expect to encounter many people who do not fully understand the finer points of project management, such as the use of ranged estimates and the need to use influence rather than authority to get things done. This will be particularly true in organizations that are just beginning to use formalized project management or have traditionally relied on a functional management approach. Take the time to educate others about projects and project management whenever you sense a knowledge gap. This practice will eventually benefit you, as others begin to better understand you and the nature of your life as a project manager.

Unfortunately, many project managers today would receive a very unfavorable response from their organizational management to that type of "crude" estimate. It doesn't provide the certainty that management requires for approval.

Unfortunately, this example is not exceptional. The uncertainty associated with projects exists throughout the life of the project: it simply never goes away—nor does management's craving for certainty.

Skill Requirements of the Project Manager

To fulfill the responsibilities described above and handle the challenges you'll face, you'll need very diverse skills and a wealth of knowledge. So what knowledge and skills does it take to be an effective project manager?

There are many ways to slice up this pie. The way that makes the most sense to me is to break it down into four major knowledge and skill categories:

1. project management process skills
2. interpersonal and behavioral skills
3. technology management skills
4. desired personal traits

Let's examine each in detail.

Project Management Process Skills

Project management process skills (sometimes called the "hard skills") are knowledge and skills related to the mechanics of project management. You should be extremely knowledgeable about project management tools, techniques, and process technology and be able to apply them. For example, you should be know how to prepare a comprehensive customer requirements document, construct a network diagram, and construct a work breakdown structure. Without these skills, you'll find it very difficult to coordinate and facilitate the creation of a high-quality project plan and to maintain control during project execution. Also, since these skills are a basic expectation, you can expect to encounter problems of respect from your team members if you're deficient in this area. As mentioned earlier, this skill set is the main focus of this book.

Interpersonal and Behavioral Skills

Since managing projects is all about getting things done through other people, your skills in dealing with people are of immeasurable value. Closely tied to your interpersonal skills are your behavioral skills: your personal conduct, style, and approach. Together, these two skill sets are often called the "soft skills." Here are some examples of soft skills:

- team and individual leadership
- oral and written communication
- conflict resolution
- negotiation
- influencing
- delegating
- coaching and mentoring

For individuals coming to project management from a highly technical background, soft skill development can be particularly challenging. Later in this chapter we'll discuss methods for developing these skills.

Technology Management Skills

Most projects have one or more *embedded technologies*. An embedded technology refers to the process or technology areas at the core of the project. Examples might include software development, chemical processing, or commercial construction. Your ability to guide and coordinate the application of these technologies is crucial to your success as a project manager. If you're like Brad, you'll probably have sufficient knowledge and skills in the primary embedded technology of the project. However, it's likely that there will be several technology areas associated with your project. Although they will differ in focus, the process steps and related skills involved in managing their successful application will be similar.

Among these technology management skills are the following:

- proficiency in project's core (primary) technology
- proficiency in supporting technology areas
- industry knowledge
- ability to prepare comprehensive technical specifications
- design skills
- product knowledge
- process knowledge
- management of intellectual property
- patent knowledge

Desired Personal Traits

Many studies have been performed to correlate personality traits to success as a project manager. Although each study reveals slightly different results, the traits shown in Figure 3-1 appear in most. Possessing these traits will stand you in good stead in your role as project manager.

Honesty and integrity	Process-oriented
Thinks like a generalist	Self-aware/reflective
High tolerance for ambiguity	Open and accessible
High tolerance for uncertainty	Politically astute
Persuasive	Decisive
Assertive	

Figure 3-1. Deiriable traits for project managers

> ### Managing Supporting Technologies   ⚠️ CAUTION! ⚠️
> Your biggest challenge in the area of technology manage-
> ment will probably come from dealing with the people
> responsible for managing the supporting technology areas. It's likely that
> they will be your peers, which could lead to some angst, jealousy, and
> competition. You can expect this interaction to test your interpersonal
> and behavioral skills as much as any other, perhaps more.

Of these personal traits, I consider the following four to be
among the most critical.

1. Thinks like a generalist—Project managers must always be
thinking in terms of the big picture. This can be a challenge
for those who are accustomed to focusing more narrowly.
Although this trait certainly requires knowledge in many different areas, what's crucial is that you must pay attention and
care about everything and everybody.

2. A high tolerance for ambiguity—This competency will be
particularly challenging if you're technically oriented. You'll
often receive mixed signals or contradictory data. You need to
develop processes for finding truth and narrowing down inputs
without getting frustrated. This will probably not be easy for
you.

3. A high tolerance for uncertainty—As with ambiguity, this is
particularly challenging if you're entering project management
from the technical arena. Most technically oriented people are
accustomed to precision. As a project manager, the norm is to
make many decisions without sufficient information. You must
condition yourself to making decisions that are only acceptable,
not perfect.

4. Honesty and integrity—Although obvious virtues, these traits
are worthy of specific mention. Whenever studies are performed
on the traits that people most admire or desire in leaders, honesty and integrity always rise to the top. One of the best behavioral traits for a project manager is to be known as doing what
you say you'll do. Closely related is the issue of integrity, having

a reputation as someone who will follow principles, even in the face of adversity or temptation.

Together, the combination of hard skills, soft skills, functional competencies, and personal traits compose the raw material for your overall capability as a project manager. But how should you develop that capability? Figure 3-2 below reveals that there's no single answer to this question.

As this figure illustrates, skills that are somewhat mechanical can be learned or developed through self-study, reading, or facilitated training and practice. Many of the hard skills fall into this category. However, as you migrate toward the soft skills, the preferred mode of development moves from programmed learning to coaching or mentoring. Here, soft skills are best developed through observation and feedback from others—preferably those in a position to do so. Further to the left in Figure 3-2 are personality traits. At the far left are those traits that make up the very fabric of your personality and affect your behavior and conduct on a very basic level, such as your belief system and moral values. On this end of the development continuum, the prospect of self-improvement becomes very personal. In fact, as you approach the far left, it's likely that you

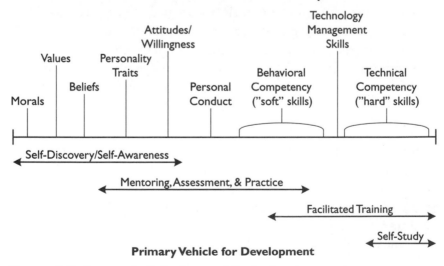

Figure 3-2. Personal attributes and their development

can develop only by being introspective—through self-examination and self-analysis. The importance of being introspective will be discussed later in this chapter.

Functional Competencies of the Project Manager

The term *functional competencies* refers to your ability to synthesize the various skills described above and properly apply them as a project manager. Even if you've very proficient in many of the skill areas, your capability as a project manager will be limited if you can't apply those skills in your day-to-day activities effectively. Figure 3-3 contains a partial list of functional competencies.

Project Management Process Functions
- Coordinates development of comprehensive, realistic, and understandable plans, estimates and budgets
- Able to balance technical solutions with business and interpersonal factors
- Develops and follows appropriate processes and procedures for accomplishing work
- Obtains formal approvals of project parameters (cost, schedule, etc.) as needed
- Monitors progress and manages deviations in a timely and effective manner
- Anticipates problems and reacts to change through a well-defined, rigorous process

Technology Management Functions
- Ensures that a rational process is used to select the appropriate technology
- Balances technology advancement needs with the need to achieve business results
- Ensures that all technical disciplines are appropriately represented on core team
- Accurately assesses the quality of most technical decisions and recommendations
- Fully utilizes and leverages all related or supporting technologies
- Effectively communicates technical information to a wide variety of people

Figure 3-3. Partial list of functional competencies for a project manager (Continued on next page)

Cognitive Functions
- Gathers information systematically; seeks input from several sources
- Considers a broad range of issues or factors when solving problems
- Collects the appropriate quantity of data for the situation before making a decision
- Draws accurate conclusions from quantitative data
- Makes decisions in an unbiased, objective manner using an appropriate process
- Understands concept of risk vs. return and makes judgments accordingly

Team Leadership Functions
- Fosters development of a common mission and vision
- Clearly defines roles, responsibilities, and performance expectations
- Uses leadership style appropriate to situation or stage of team development
- Fosters collaboration among team members
- Provides clear direction and priorities
- Removes obstacles that impede team progress, readiness, or effectiveness
- Promotes team participation in problem solving and decision making as appropriate
- Passes credit on to team; promotes their positive visibility to upper management
- Appreciates, promotes, and leverages the diversity within the team

Interpersonal Relationship Functions
- Adjusts approach to individual situations as personalities dictate
- Communicates effectively with all levels inside and outside of the organization
- Negotiates fairly and effectively
- Brings conflict into the open and manages it collaboratively and productively
- Able to influence without relying on coercive power or threats
- Conveys ideas and information clearly and concisely, both in writing and orally

Self-Management Functions
- Maintains focus and control when faced with ambiguity and uncertainty
- Shows consistency among principles, values, and behavior
- Resilient and tenacious in the face of pressure, opposition, constraints, or adversity

Figure 3-3. Continued

- Manages implementation effectively; recognized as someone who "gets things done"
- Actively seeks feedback and modifies behavior accordingly
- Actively pursues learning and self-development opportunities

Motivational and Personal Development Functions

- Considers individual's skills, values, and interests when assigning or delegating tasks
- Allows team members an appropriate amount of freedom to do the job
- Accurately assesses individuals' strengths and development needs
- Continually seeks and offers opportunities for personal and professional growth
- Provides for training and support when needed
- Passes credit on to individuals; promotes their positive visibility to upper management
- Seeks to understand what drives individuals' behavior before trying to modify it
- Gives timely, specific, and constructive feedback

Customer Awareness Functions

- Anticipates customer's needs and proactively strives to satisfy them
- Accurately "translates" the customer's verbalized wants into what they actually need
- Seeks to understand customers and their business
- Actively builds and maintains strong customer relationships
- Responsive to customer's issues, concerns, and queries
- Actively strives to exceed customer expectations

Organizational Savvy Functions

- Involves the right people at the right time
- Understands, accepts, and properly uses power and influence in relationships
- Builds and leverages formal and informal networks to get things done
- Knows the mission, structure, and functions of their organization and others
- Understands profitability and general management philosophy
- Understands how project management is regarded in their company or organization
- Balances interests and needs of team/project with those of the broader organization

Figure 3-3. Concluded

The Project Manager's "Unofficial" Job Duties

The functional competencies listed in Figure 3-3 represent *official duties* of the typical project manager. In fact, if your organization has developed a job description for project managers, it probably includes many of these functional competencies. What you won't find in job descriptions are the unofficial duties that project managers perform in the course of carrying out their mission. Let's examine some of the key ones (somewhat tongue in cheek).

Babysitter—This refers to the apparent need to provide close guidance or detailed instructions to certain individuals. This situation results from any number of root causes. The target may be underqualified, lack confidence, or simply crave attention.

Salesperson—There will be times when you'll have to rely heavily on your ability to influence others to sell an idea, sell yourself, or perhaps sell the virtues of project management. Most of your selling situations will be helpful and have positive outcomes. However, if you find yourself spending too much time selling project management, that may signal deeper underlying problems, such as issues of trust or confidence. If most of the selling you do is to your management, you're in trouble. This is a signal that your life as a project manager may be exceptionally challenging.

Teacher—This is an example of an unofficial role that actually yields positive results. In fact, superior project managers will be able to educate and develop those they work with as they manage the project. Acquire this skill or reputation and you'll be in very good shape.

Friend—Maintaining friendships and professional relationships with the same people is difficult. However, if you can do it, you'll benefit greatly. In Chapter 2, we discussed the value of the informal network of communication. An open, informal, and comfortable communication linkage is much more likely to keep you supplied with more of the information you need than formal, rigorous, and stiff team meetings. Finally, avoid the trap of believing that because you've been put "in charge" of a project you've risen above your peers and friendships no longer matter. Big mistake!

The Value of Introspection and Self-Awareness to "The Soft Side"

As mentioned above, you'll have to take charge of some of your growth and development as a project manager. This is particularly true in the areas of beliefs, values, and some personality traits—the softest of the soft skills. Some project managers make the mistake of believing that simply because they're constantly surrounded by others they'll receive continuous feedback on their performance and behavior. This is simply not true.

Why not? Consider the groups of project players who surround you in the course of executing your project and the likelihood of getting high-quality feedback from that group.

Project Team Members—Although we've said that you don't have formal authority over team members, there remains the sense that you have some control over their destiny. So, the

Eight Key Tips for Success as a Project Manager Tricks of the Trade

Many people ask me this: "If you could list a few key tips for good project management, what would they be"? Here's how I answer that question...

1. Care about everything; dwell on nothing.
2. Don't wait to be told to do something.
3. Develop a keen understanding of human nature.
4. Learn the who, when, and how of relying on others.
5. Consider technology, people, and business when making decisions.
6. Learn how to make decisions with ambiguous, imperfect, or incomplete information.
7. Never stop developing your social skills.
8. Appreciate the value of being politically savvy.

chances of receiving negative feedback (likely of greatest value to you) are pretty slim.

Customer—It's always nice to get positive feedback from a customer. However, they often provide it without knowing much about your day-to-day behavior and ordinarily it is based more on what they see you achieve than your ongoing performance. In addition, your relationship with clients tends to be somewhat artificial: let's face it—you always try to put your best foot forward when interacting with customers.

Your Supervisor or Manager—They don't know what you do or how you get it done. Does that sound familiar? That's one of the biggest complaints I hear about direct supervisors. What's the point? The point is simply this: the closer you get to the soft end of the competency continuum (Figure 3-3), the more you'll need to rely on yourself for self-improvement. Reflect on how you just interacted with that team member when you offered constructive feedback. Think about how you may have biases that are affecting the way you perform. Be objective about how you tend to jump to conclusions about people and how that impairs your ability to remain objective. These are examples of introspection and self-awareness.

There's an exception to the recommendation to rely on yourself for self-improvement, however. If you're fortunate enough to work with someone (a) whom you trust implicitly, (b) whose opinion you value, (c) from whom you can expect honest feedback, and (d) who is in a position to observe your on-the-job behavior, I suggest you latch onto that person and try to enlist his or her support in your quest for self-understanding. Unfortunately, the combination of all four of these factors is rare.

Now that you completely understand everything there is to know about projects, project management, and the role of the project manager, I think you're ready to move on to defining the project. So, let's get back to Brad as he prepares to launch Project Apex.

Project Manager's Checklist for Chapter 3

❏ As a project manager, you have responsibilities in four broad areas: the project, your organization, your team, and yourself.

❏ One of the unspoken roles you can perform is to educate others in what project management is all about and how it works. Doing this will actually benefit you in the long run— the more people understand project management, the smoother your life as a project manager is likely to be.

❏ The skill requirements of project managers are very diverse and include: process skills (project management tools and techniques), interpersonal and behavioral skills (getting along with and leading people), technology management skills (familiarity with technologies used in the project), and desired personal traits (your attitudes, values, and personal conduct). You need to be good in each of these areas to be highly successful.

❏ You will probably have to perform a number of "unofficial" job duties in your role as project manager. Included in the list may be babysitter, salesperson, teacher, and politician. How often you need to perform these roles will depend on who you work with and your organizational culture.

❏ Although you are continuously surrounded by potential sources of feedback (e.g., team members, customers, and peers), you can't necessarily count on them for honest, accurate feedback on your performance. You will have to learn to take charge of your self-development. Develop the ability to examine your performance and look for opportunities for improvement.

Defining
Your Project

After some brief soul-searching, Brad has determined that he's mentally prepared to take on his new role as project manager. He believes he understands what's involved in the role and is very eager to begin work. So is Susan, who has just called him into her office. As she hands him a folder, Susan says, "Brad, here are the requirements for Project Apex. They were developed by our Operations folks, with a little help from Marketing. I'd like you to get going on this project right away, OK?"

As Brad fans through the surprisingly thick folder, Susan remarks, "Good luck, Brad. Oh, by the way," she adds, "if you should have any questions or need anything at any time during the project, please know that my door is always open."

"Thank you, Susan," Brad answers. "I'm sure I'll do a great job on Project Apex."

He turns and immediately heads back to his office, where he starts leafing through the project requirements folder. The requirements state that an additional production line is to be installed in the manufacturing department. There's also some information on a new procurement procedure that needs to be put into place. It gives some information on when the project should be completed and how much it will cost. There are also several charts that outline performance capabilities for the new line.

As Brad continues perusing the project requirements, he begins to feel more and more troubled. Something's missing, Brad thinks to himself. It finally hits him and he begins muttering, "What's the problem here? I don't understand. I see that they want me to put in a new production line and do some other stuff. That seems clear enough. But *why* am I putting in the production line?

"Oh, great," he groans. "A project manager for less than 20 minutes and I'm already encountering a crisis!"

How Projects Should Evolve

Brad should not feel badly about being confused. He's troubled because he's fallen victim to a problem that's common in many matrix organizations. Someone from another department has defined the solution to a problem, then "thrown it over the wall" to Brad. Brad doesn't know what the original problem is and whether the project he's been given is the best way to solve it. Among other things, he feels that he'd like to know whether a valid process was used to define the project.

And that's OK. As a matter of fact, that's something you should do on your projects. So let's help Brad by describing how projects *should* evolve, so he can better understand the situation he's in and ask the right questions.

Projects typically begin when we recognize that a need exists. From this point on, however, we can often become our own worst enemies—and can lose control very rapidly—if we don't follow a disciplined approach. Why? Because we're human. When any of us spots a problem, our natural tendency is to want to solve it right away—*often with the first solution that pops into our heads*. That's just human nature. On the surface, this approach may seem admirable, because it seems to resolve problems swiftly and decisively. Unfortunately, it's counterproductive to good project management. A solid approach for getting your project off the ground consists of faithfully following four basic steps.

1. Fully understand the problem or opportunity. Problems are ordinarily complex, consisting of many aspects that require analysis and insight. There's frequently more to a problem than what's apparent at first blush. We need to invest an appropriate amount of time to fully understand all aspects of the problem. Very often, what appears to be the problem is actually masking a bigger, more fundamental problem. Uncovering that fundamental problem is referred to as *identifying the true need.*

> **MISTAKE PROOFING**
>
> ### Identifying the Client's True Need
>
> Identifying the client's true need—the most fundamental problem or opportunity—is the first and the most important step in the entire project process.

2. Identify the optimum solution. The solutions we identify through our initial, "knee-jerk" response—though they might work to solve the problem—may not be the most effective. For many problems, there are multiple solutions and various approaches for carrying them out. The key to effective project management is to determine the *best* solution—the one that's most attractive to the organization. This requires some careful thought and the development of criteria by which we can evaluate which solution is "best."

3. Fully develop the solution and a preliminary plan. When a solution is identified, it's typically characterized in one or two brief statements (install an additional production line, for example). This solution statement must be converted into a plan. The process begins with a full description of the solution, including the methods for achieving it. It ends with the development of a credible, detailed project plan that the team can use as a map for execution.

4. Formally launch the project. The activities involved in the formal initiation of project execution depend on the organization's specific project procedures. Project launch activities may include preparing a business case, making formal presentations to management, creating and approving a project charter, and securing funding to proceed. It also should include team-oriented activities, such as conducting a kickoff meeting and establishing mutual expectations between you and your project team.

Let's take a closer look at each of the steps required to properly define and launch a project.

First, Fully Understand the Problem or Opportunity

Problems and opportunities can arise almost anywhere inside or outside the organization. Problems are typically driven from within and frequently relate to improving organizational performance. For example:

- A department that's overwhelmed with paperwork may need to simplify its procedures.
- An organization that constantly faces the prospect of worker strikes may very much need to improve management/employee relations.
- An insurance company that has branch locations spread across a wide geographic region may need to communicate effectively among branches.

Problems are generally regarded as negative. Opportunities may be viewed as their positive alter ego. Opportunities are often driven by external forces. One of the more common examples of opportunities can be found in the areas of product development or product enhancement. These opportunities are often the response to a perceived need in the marketplace.

Uncovering Problems and Opportunities
Smart Managing

The recognition of *needs*—whether problems or opportunities—requires conscious effort. Constantly ask, "What are our needs?" and "What are the needs of our clients?" Establish procedures for systematically identifying needs. Focus attention not only on existing needs, but also on anticipated needs.

Identifying the True Need

The term "true need" refers to the most basic problem to be solved. Identifying your project's true need can, at times, be tricky. But it's absolutely vital that you as the project manager understand what the true need is.

Why? Because *many will judge you as a project manager by your ability to solve the original problem.* Solving the original problem equates to satisfying the true need. And you cannot be certain that you'll satisfy the true need unless you know what it is. The problem is that when you're assigned to manage a project you may not be presented with the true need explicitly. Terminology can become confused: what's described as a need may actually be the solution to a need.

This is exactly what happened to Brad. What the "requirements" document identified as a need—namely, to install an additional production line—was actually a solution. Though Brad senses this intuitively, Figure 4-1 lists indicators that could have helped him verify his intuition.

Most books on project management deal only with the "mechanics" of managing projects and helping you manage the project you've been assigned. However, properly identifying and quantifying the true need is actually more important than plan-

A Customer REQUIREMENT (the need):	A Proposed SOLUTION (the project):
Describes the necessary *client's* **ends**.	Describes the *team's* **means** to the ends.
Specifies goals and targets; *does not identify how* to achieve them.	Develops specific strategies and detailed ideas for achieving the goals and targets.
Leaves open the question as to "how to do it."	*Closes* the door on the question of "how to do it."
The answer to "why are we doing it" should yield the *business justification*.	The answer to "why we are doing it" should yield the *customer requirements*.

Figure 4-1. Indicators that verify intuition about a project

ning and executing the project. It's often been said that it doesn't matter how well you manage your project if you aren't working on the right thing. Bill found this out the hard way in Chapter 2 when he was assigned to solve Amy's problem.

One of the most reliable methods for uncovering the true need is to ask the right people one simple question: "Why?"

However, as you seek to uncover the true need, you can expect to encounter some resistance.

If you ask questions rather than digging in and getting the project going, some within your organization may assume that you're not moving forward. However, asking the right questions of the right peo-

> ### Treading on Thin Ice
>
> **CAUTION!**
>
> As you seek to understand what the client's true need is, some people may feel threatened or offended, as it may appear that you're questioning the judgment of those who were involved prior to your assignment. Make sure that everyone understands that this is not your intent.

ple can often lead to some startling discoveries, as Brad finds out when he decides to do a little investigating ....

Bothered that he doesn't understand the purpose for Project Apex, Brad returns to Susan's office and asks, "Susan, can you tell me *why* we're putting in this production line?"

Susan thinks for a moment. "No, I can't," she replies. "But Bill in Operations might be able to tell you."

"Thanks very much, Susan," Brad says as he exits her office. Later that day, Brad gets the opportunity to sit down with Bill in Operations and asks him the same question.

"Bill, can you tell me *why* you need an additional production line?"

Bill looks quizzical. "Why are you asking, Brad? I don't understand why you're asking."

"I'd just like to try to understand the project a bit better," Brad responds.

"OK," says Bill, reluctantly. "Well, we need another production line because we can't meet the growing demand with the four lines we have now." Then he adds, "When we put these lines in four years ago, we were anticipating an output of about 800 units per week, but they only got the output up to 600 when we had to go online. It wasn't a problem until recently, when we realized we would fall short of demand by the end of the year. That's why you have to put another line in right away."

Brad feels as if he's one step closer to identifying the true need. Then, in a bold move, he decides to try the magic question one more time. "*Why* are you only getting 600 units per week, Bill?"

At this point, Bill has obviously had enough. "If you need anymore information, go talk to Ann. She's the engineer who put these lines in."

As Brad is leaving, Bill repeats, "Brad, we *really* need you to get going on this new line right away, OK?" Brad just nods and smiles.

Before setting up an appointment with Ann, Brad decides to reflect on the situation. The "need" presented to him is to install a production line in Operations. But his talk with Bill revealed that the true need is that they would not be able to meet demand by the end of the year, because they're not getting the anticipated output from their existing production lines. It doesn't take Brad long to figure out that if he can improve the efficiency of the production lines from 600 units per week to 800 units per week, his client may be able to avoid putting in a brand new production line. Brad senses a potential opportunity and picks up the phone to call Ann.

Brad's experience is not uncommon in the process of identifying and understanding true needs. It represents an excellent example of the phenomenon of *solution-jumping*. As described in Chapter 2, this is when we grab at the first or most obvious solution to a problem. In this case, since the four existing lines could not meet demand, someone determined that a fifth line was needed. Brad recognizes that installing a fifth production line would satisfy the need to meet demand, but may not represent the optimum solution. As Brad has discovered, the only way to be sure we've identified the best solution is to be sure we fully understand and articulate the need. This is the function of the Project Requirements Document.

Preparing the Project Requirements Document

Once you've identified the true need, you need to expand upon it and fully quantify it. You should capture your elaboration of the true need in one of the most basic project management documents—the *requirements document* (or *client requirements document*). The length of the requirements document can vary from one to several pages.

The following items should be included in a comprehensive requirements document.

> **Requirements Document Etiquette**
> A properly written Requirements Document should never offer a solution; it should only describe a need. (Refer back to Figure 4-1.)

- **Description of the problem or opportunity.** This is ordinarily a narrative that describes in several sentences the problem to be solved, the deficiency that's been discovered, or the opportunity that could be exploited. It might also describe *how* the need was discovered.
- **Impact or effects of the problem.** This is a brief description of the types of difficulties encountered because of the problem or because the opportunity has not been addressed.
- **Identification of who or what is affected by the problem.** This may be stated in terms of individuals, departments, or organizations.
- **Impact of ignoring the problem or opportunity.** This is a statement that is intended to describe what will happen if the need is not addressed, which is also known as *inaction risk*.
- **Desired outcome.** This is a description of what we would like the world to look like if the project is successful. It's ordinarily stated in terms of objectives, critical success factors, and, in some cases, deliverables.

- **Value or benefit associated with achieving desired outcome.** This is ordinarily broken down into two major categories: financial benefits and non-financial benefits. Non-financial benefits are sometimes called the *intangibles.*
- **Strategic fit.** This part is intended to address the question, "Is the pursuit or is the execution of this project going to be compatible with our current set of company or organizational strategies?" This is particularly relevant for opportunities.
- **Interface integration and compatibility issues.** This describes how this project opportunity or the satisfaction of these objectives may relate to other aspects of the organization.
- **Uncertainties and unknowns.** Also known as *action risk,* this part represents the early stages of risk management. Any unknowns, uncertainties, or threats would be identified here.
- **Key assumptions.** Assumptions ordinarily take the place of missing information. They represent anticipated values or conditions that we may or may not know to be true.
- **Constraints.** Constraints are limitations within which the solution must be executed. Constraints may come in many forms, including time, funding, resources, technology, or procedural constraints.
- **Environmental considerations.** This part is for potential impacts or effects that this project may have beyond the boundaries of the project itself. Some categories of environmental considerations include business, marketing, operational, and technical.
- **Background or supporting information.** This is essentially a repository for all of the information or research that has led us up to this point. It may include historical data, results of supporting studies, tests or survey data, marketing situational analysis, benchmarking data, or prototype test results, to name a few examples.

Reality Check #1: Stop or Go?

Although it is very early in the life of the project, two important questions should be asked:

- Is this problem worth solving?
- Does a potential solution exist?

These two questions address the issues of *justification* and *feasibility*, respectively. You should address both issues before continuing. If not, you run the risk of wasting time and money on problems that should not or cannot be solved.

Justification—particularly *financial justification*—is very difficult to assess at the requirements stage, because not much is really known about the project. Nonetheless, it's wise to try to assess whether or not you can justify continuing the project. You may be able to do this by executing a simple cost vs. benefit analysis.

The benefit component is relatively easy to estimate: it's the *value of satisfying the need*. In many cases, this is nothing more than calculating how much the problem is costing today. Estimating the cost of the solution is more difficult, because you're not sure what you're going to do or how you're going to do it. One approach you may wish to consider consists of working backwards through the financial calculations. (We'll cover these later in this chapter.) By doing this, you can determine the most you'd be able to spend on a solution. If none of your proposed solutions can be executed for less than that amount of money, the project will ultimately be unjustifiable—at least from a purely financial standpoint.

The second issue, feasibility, comes down to a basic question: Do you believe that a solution exists? In other words, can this problem even be solved? This step is referred to *verifying feasibility*. There can be much subjectivity in this step; you should rely heavily on the judgment of subject matter experts. In reality, the most that you can realistically hope to determine at this point is that the *possibility* of a solution is thought to exist. That's OK. As with justification, all you're trying to do at this point is preclude the expenditure of additional resources and money on problems that have no reasonable solution.

Second, Identify the Optimum Solution

Once you fully understand the need and establish that satisfying the need is justifiable and feasible, you're ready to determine the best way to satisfy that need. Although I'm using the term "you," proper execution of this step really requires the input of many individuals. If you're fortunate enough to be involved at this stage of the project's evolution (remember, Brad was not!), you should be actively working toward building a team that can work with you from this point on.

Identifying Alternative Solutions

The process of identifying the optimal way to satisfy the project requirements begins with generating a list of *potential solutions.* This process can be greatly enhanced in the following ways:

- Do it in a team environment.
- Include subject matter experts and stakeholders as appropriate.
- Use brainstorming techniques.
- Limit further development to only reasonable alternatives.

Brainstorming

Brainstorming is a group-oriented technique that involves the spontaneous contribution of ideas from all members of a team or group. Ground rules for conducting a productive brainstorming session include the following:

- Stress the quantity of ideas vs. quality.
- Encourage every member of the group to contribute any and all ideas.
- Do not be concerned with reasonableness or feasibility initially.
- Do not criticize, judge or evaluate contributions until you are done.
- Encourage the practice of combining or modifying ideas already identified.

Selecting the Best Alternative

Obviously, you can't pursue every idea identified through processes like brainstorming. After soliciting all reasonable alternative solutions, the project team needs to pare the list down to only those that are worthy of further development, investigation, and definition. You can reduce the list by comparing each alternative against predetermined criteria.

This is where the Requirements Document begins to add significant value. The process for selecting the optimum solution begins by evaluating each alternative solution in terms of how well it satisfies the most critical aspects of the project requirements, such as budget constraints or strategic alignment. You may also wish to use other requirements-based considerations, such as the likelihood of technical success or the anticipated impact on existing products. This initial screening will allow you to shorten the list of potential alternative solutions to a manageable number—I would recommend two to five.

At this point, the selection process becomes much more rigorous. Each potential alternative should be evaluated using two basic types of criteria: financial and non-financial.

Using Financial Criteria for Project Selection

Companies that use project selection and justification methods often rely on financial calculations as a comparative tool and as a basic hurdle for management approval. Basic financial evaluation models—variously known as financial analysis, business case, project financials, or cost/benefit analysis—often include some combination of these four basic metrics: net present value, internal rate of return, payback period, and cash hole. Let's take a look at each of these metrics in more detail.

- **Net present value (NPV).** Calculating a project's NPV answers the question: How much money will this project make (or save)? It's a calculation in dollars of the *present value of all future cash flows* expected from a project. It's *roughly* analogous to the concept of profit.

> **Key Term**
>
> **Net present value** The value in present dollars of all cash flows expected in the future from a project.
>
> **Internal rate of return** The percentage rate at which the project will bring a return on the investment.
>
> **Payback period** Also known as *time to money* or *breakeven point,* the number of months or years the project will take to recover the original investment.
>
> **Cash hole** Also known as the *maximum exposure,* the most money that will be invested in the project at any point.

- **Internal rate of return (IRR).** Calculating the IRR answers the question: How rapidly will the money be returned? It's a calculation of the percentage rate at which the project will return wealth. It's *roughly* analogous to the effective yield of a savings account.
- **Payback period.** Calculating this metric (also known as *time to money* or *breakeven point*) answers the question: When will the original investment (the amount spent on the project) be recovered through benefits? It's typically expressed in months or years.
- **Cash hole.** Calculating the cash hole (also known as the *maximum exposure*) answers the question: What's the most we'll have invested at any given point in time? It's expressed in terms of dollars.

Performing a Financial Analysis (or Cost vs. Benefit Analysis)

Each of the four financial metrics identified above can be determined by performing a *financial analysis.* Although you may not be intimately involved in performing a complete financial analysis, as a savvy project manager you should understand how it's done and the terminology involved. The basic financial analysis process is not as difficult as many think. It consists of four basic steps.

Step 1: Identify the Sources of Cash Flows (Inflows and Outflows). Executing a project causes money to flow out and in. Cash *inflows* are any *financial* benefits that can be claimed as a result of executing your project: e.g., an increase in revenue from sales, a reduction in production or operating costs, material savings, and waste reduction. Cash *outflows* are any erxpenditures or losses due to the project or its downstream effects. The most obvious cash outflow is the cost of the project itself. However, an increase in operating costs due to the project would also be a cash outflow.

Step 2: Estimate the Magnitude of Specific Cash Flows. In some cases, it will be fairly straightforward to estimate cash flows. In other cases, it may be very difficult. For example, consider how confident you would feel in placing a *specific dollar value* on these benefits:

- Increased output due to enhanced employee satisfaction
- Improvement in vendor delivery reliability
- Improvement in workforce safety
   Increase in user comfort or convenience
- Reduction in potential legal action against your organization

In estimating some of these types of cash flows, it can be very useful to rely on historical data or benchmark data.

Step 3: Chart the Cash Flows. After you've estimated the magnitude of all cash flows, you can construct a cash flow diagram (such as the one in Figure 4-2). You should chart all cash outflows and inflows year by year throughout the useful life of the project.

At the bottom of the cash flow diagram are the year-by-year cash flow totals and the cumulative cash flows throughout the useful life of the project.

Useful life The period of time over which the financial analysis will be conducted. Although it's related to factors such as the anticipated working life of an asset or the expected size of a market window, it's actually a value that your accounting department establishes.

The final step consists of making an allowance for the *time value of money*.

	YEAR after project initiation									
	1	2	3	4	5	6	7	8	9	10
Cash Outflows										
R&D Costs	-40	-20								
Capital Costs		-80	-60							
Operating Costs				-40	-40	-40	-40	-40	-40	-40
Cash Inflows										
Sales				+80	+80	+80	+80	+80	+80	+80
Maintenance				+15	+15	+15	+15	+15	+15	+15
Materials				+10	+10	+10	+10	+10	+10	+10
Waste				+5	+5	+5	+5	+5	+5	+5
Cash Flow/Year	-40	-100	-60	+70	+70	+70	+70	+70	+70	+70
Discounted Cash Flow/Year	-40	-91	-50	+53	+48	+43	+40	+36	+33	+30
Cumulative Discounted Cash Flow	-40	-131	-181	-128	-80	-37	+3	+39	+72	+102

Figure 4-2. Cash flow diagram (all dollars in 000s)

Step 4: Calculate the Net Cash Flow Using an Agreed-upon Discount Rate. Because the value of a dollar in the future is less than the value of a dollar today, the value of future cash flows must discounted using the formula shown in Figure 4-3. The letter "r" is the *discount rate, cost of capital,* or *required return*—is, in simple terms, what the investor (your company) could expect to receive from any other investment that is consistent with its risk tolerance. Ordinarily, the company's financial department establishes the discount rate.

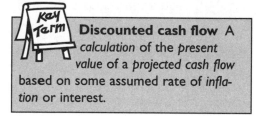

Discounted cash flow A *calculation* of the *present value* of a *projected cash flow* based on some assumed rate of *inflation* or interest.

By using this formula, you can easily calculate the net present value of any project. An NPV greater than zero indicates that your project is expected to provide a financial return that exceeds the

$$NPV = \frac{Cash\ Flow_{Year\ 0}}{(1+r)^0} + \frac{Cash\ Flow_{Year\ 1}}{(1+r)^1} + \frac{Cash\ Flow_{Year\ 2}}{(1+r)^2} + \cdots \frac{Cash\ Flow_{Year\ n}}{(1+r)^n}$$

Where
n = Useful life of investment
r = the discount rate, cost of capital, or required return that is what
    the investor could expect to receive from any other investment
    consistent with investor's risk tolerance

Figure 4-3. Formula for finding NPV

organization's investment expectations, so your project is likely to be approved (if there's enough cash to fund it).

To calculate the internal rate of return, use the same formula. However, set NPV to zero and solve the equation for "r." The resulting figure, expressed in terms of a percentage, represents the effective yield that your project will bring to your organization.

The third financial metric, payback period or time to money, occurs when the cumulative discounted cash flow is zero, signaling the return of the original investment (as shown in Figure 4-2). In this example, the payback period ends between years six and seven.

Finally, the cash hole or maximum exposure occurs at the point where the cumulative negative cash flow is greatest. In the example shown in Figure 4-2, the maximum exposure is expected to be $181,000, three years after project initiation.

Using Non-Financial Criteria for Project Selection

Financial models express costs and benefits in dollars and cents. As mentioned earlier, estimating certain kinds of benefits in financial terms can be quite difficult or uncomfortable. In other situations, accurate data may be obtainable, but only by conducting expensive tests, studies, or surveys. *Whenever the process of getting good financial data is difficult, expensive, or time-consuming, using a weighted factor scoring model (decision matrix) may be a reasonable option for selecting the best alternative solution.*

Figure 4-4 shows a decision matrix constructed to determine the preferred model of automobile. We've identified six

Alter-native	Attributes (Realtive Weighting)						Total Score
	Cost (.15)	Comfort (.25)	Style (.10)	Handling (.15)	Reliability (.20)	Resale (.10)	
Olds 98	3 / .45	2 / .50	2 / .20	5 / .75	4 / .80	3 / .45	3.1
Cadillac deVille	1 / .15	4 / 1.00	2 / .20	4 / .60	4 / .80	3 / .45	3.2
Lincoln Town Car	2 / .30	3 / .75	4 / .40	4 / .60	4 / .80	4 / .60	3.4
Mercury Marquis	2 / .30	3 / .75	1 / .10	5 / .75	3 / .60	3 / .45	2.9

Figure 4-4. Example of decision matrix

attributes that are meaningful to us: cost, comfort, style, handling, reliability, and resale. We then weight each attribute by assessing a relative importance to it. The weights must total 1.

Weighted Factor Scoring Model

The weighted factor scoring model (decision matrix) is a comparative method for selecting the preferred alternative based upon certain predetermined attributes. Although it does not provide absolute verification of justification, it offers a method for selecting among alternatives.

To use a decision matrix, you need to establish a scale for rating each alternative for each attribute. (The example shown uses a five-point rating scale.) You must define the scale so that everyone has a common understanding of what each rating number—0, 1, 2, 3, 4, 5—represents. Once you've established the relative weighting and the rating scale, it's merely a question of filling in the blanks to determine the best alternative. In our example, using six weighted attributes and a five-point scale, the Lincoln Town Car was determined to be the best alternative.

Use of a weighted factor scoring model offers several advantages:

- It allows for using multiple criteria, including financial data. The attributes you select could include any combination of the four financial metrics presented in this chapter.

- It is easy to construct and to interpret.
- It allows for management input. Management can determine the appropriate attributes and the relative weighting. In fact, involving management in constructing the matrix may streamline the project approval process.
- It is well suited to *what-if studies* and *sensitivity analysis*. Trade-offs between criteria are readily observable.

There are also some disadvantages:

- The process relies almost entirely upon subjective measure, thus opening it up to questions of bias, halo effects, and reliance on opinion or judgment.
- The result obtained is only a measure of *relative attractiveness*. There is no absolute verification that any of the alternatives identified is a justifiable investment from a business perspective.
- All attributes are assumed to be independent; there are no allowances made for interdependencies between or among factors.

> **Use Financial and Non-Financial Criteria**   TRICKS OF THE TRADE
>
> Considering both financial and non-financial criteria is an excellent way to ensure a comprehensive analysis of alternative solutions. Use a weighted factor scoring model and include only alternatives that are financially justifiable. Include one or more of the financial metrics as attributes. You can vary their relative weight according to how dominant you want financial criteria to be.

Reality Check #2: Stop or Go?

Once a specific alternative has been identified, you should verify justification and feasibility again. The question of justification should have been addressed by performing the financial calculations above. Feasibility can now be evaluated much more readily than during the requirements stage, since you now know what the solution is. Methods for verifying feasibility include market studies, pilot testing, prototyping, and simulation. Let's examine each method.

Market Studies. If your project is to bring a new product to market, you must determine its market potential. Market research asks customers whether your product satisfies their current or potential perceived needs. It can also examine similar products to determine how your product is differentiated.

Pilot Testing. You can try out your project on a small scale, such as in a limited area market test of a product or a working model of key project deliverables. Sometimes known as *field testing*, a pilot test gives you the opportunity to observe your project's performance under actual conditions.

Prototyping. This is constructing and assembling some portion of the project deliverable or deliverables and putting them through performance tests designed to verify whether or not they can meet the performance criteria identified in the requirements.

Simulation. Computer technology permits modeling of many types of projects. For example, you can predict the market potential of a product by analyzing demographic data of the target users along with assumptions about current and potential needs or you can determine the load-bearing potential of buildings, bridges, and vessels through mathematical calculations and computer simulation. The value of simulations lies in their ability to identify potential problems in a risk-free environment.

If the results of a well-conceived and executed feasibility study indicate that the project should proceed, you can move confidently into the planning and implementation phases. If the results are discouraging, you can use the data to redesign the project and do another feasibility study, and so on, until you've identified a project concept that works.

Third, Fully Develop the Solution and a Preliminary Plan

At this point, you've identified the preferred solution. Now, you need to develop the details. This step consists of completely defining every aspect of the preferred solution. It's a progressive elaboration of the work to be done, beginning with the *Project Definition Document.*

Preparing the Project Definition Document

The Project Definition Document takes the project alternative that you've selected to the next level of detail. You could think of the Project Definition Document as the "response" to the Project Requirements Document. Several names are used for this document, including Project Objective Statement, Project Scope Statement, and Statement of Work Document. Whatever the name, the objective is the same: to initiate the process of fully defining the work to be done. This information then becomes the basis for all future planning documentation.

The Project Definition Document serves many purposes:

- It identifies what work will be done and how it will be done.
- During planning, it forces stakeholders to agree on the boundaries of the project scope.
- During execution, it enables identification of changes that fall outside the boundaries and would therefore require renegotiation of the original contract.
- It helps you establish completion criteria to which all involved can agree.
- It helps you establish success criteria to which all involved can agree.
- It helps the team agree on the approaches and methods to use.
- It facilitates widespread understanding of what the project will not include.

Though the primary purpose of the Project Definition Document is to describe work, it may include other information to make it more comprehensive. Normally those items are just carried over from the Project Proposal phase described above.

A comprehensive Project Definition Document should include these elements:

Problem need or opportunity. A brief high-level summary of key parts of the Project Requirements Document.

Proposed solution. Generally, this is the project title expanded for greater clarity and understanding.

Statement of work and strategy for execution. A narrative delineation of the work that will be done and descriptions of how it will be done. It must be stated in sufficient detail to enable the breakdown of work to the task level. It should describe the general approaches and strategies for meeting project objectives. It may describe how the elements are interrelated or describe a rough sequence of how major elements of work will be carried out. This section is the primary focus of the Project Definition Document.

Major deliverables. Describes outputs or end products of the project. The level of detail in this section could vary from a general description of major outputs to a set of performance specifications.

Completion criteria. A description of what must be accomplished or delivered in order to fulfill the contract.

Risks, uncertainties, and unknowns. Identification of factors or conditions for which information is missing and that may affect the accuracy of your predictions for the project. Emphasis is ordinarily put on areas where the project may be negatively impacted relative to stakeholder expectations.

Assumptions. Information, data, or statements about conditions that have unknown validity, used when there are significant unknowns or uncertainties.

A Project Definition Document *may* also include these elements:

Preliminary execution plan. Includes whatever planning documentation exists at that time, such as preliminary cost and schedule estimates, a procurement strategy, and an organizational chart of the project team, showing the functional areas involved. Since these are not fully developed plans and estimates, it's important to give any estimates in terms of ranges and to note confidence levels where it makes sense to do so, to show that any information you provide reflects your level of knowledge at this stage of the project.

Project stakeholders. A listing of individuals and organizations involved in the project or affected by the activities and/or outcomes.

Success criteria. The methods that will be used to determine how well the project objectives were met. It should include a list of critical success factors and quantified levels of achievement.

Preliminary Planning: How Much Is Enough?

You'll find this to be one of the most difficult points in the life of the project. In

> ### Obtaining Formal Agreement on Project Definition
> Smart Managing
>
> Treating the Project Definition Document as a kind of contract can be of value. It can serve to ensure that all major parties affected by the project or its outcome agree—in advance—on what is to be done and how. It's advisable to get all of these parties to formally sign off on the Project Definition Document, indicating that all are in agreement on your approach.

Chapter 1, we discussed the fundamental gap between the certainty desired by management and the inherent uncertainty of projects. This is typically the point at which that gap is greatest. You're about to make a specific project proposal to management, who will crave precise estimates. You won't be able to provide precise estimates, because you simply don't know enough at this point. You've done a limited amount of analysis, so you can't predict an outcome with much confidence.

The schedule you produce in your preliminary planning should be relatively very simple and not very detailed. In fact, the level of detail in all of your documentation should reflect your level of knowledge and certainty. In most cases, you may

Hedging Against Uncertainty

TRICKS OF THE TRADE In the preliminary planning stage, particularly in anticipation of providing a proposal to management for formal approval and authorization to proceed, consider the following tips:

1. Indicate any estimates that you make in terms of ranges of possible outcomes. For example, instead of saying that your project will cost $500,000, say that the project costs will fall somewhere in the range of $400,000 to $600,000, and instead of saying the project will be completed in 17 months, say instead 16 to 19 months.
2. Keep any graphics that you produce relatively simple. Avoid detailed graphics that suggest a higher level of knowledge or precision.
3. Clearly identify on any documents that you produce that they are preliminary.

Applying these techniques will serve to alert management and other stakeholders that your level of precision and confidence at this point is not very high.

wish only to indicate the major phases of the program and to identify some high-level milestones. Again, you should try to indicate a completion date and a cost estimate in terms of ranges, not specifics.

Figuring Out Who Can and Will Do the Work

Before presenting your project proposal to management, you should try to gain some assurance that the labor and materials required for the project will be available, should you get approval. Nothing is worse than managing a project without the proper resources. You should normally begin the process by searching within your organization and asking a few key questions:

1. Do we have people with the necessary expertise to do the work?
2. Are they willing to commit to doing the work, barring any scheduling problems?
3. Would we achieve a better result by going outside the company, such as a lower cost, higher quality, or faster delivery?
4. Are there concerns associated with going outside the organization, such as confidentiality and safety?

You can also conduct a preliminary make-or-buy analysis, which helps to determine whether it's better to obtain a deliverable or group of deliverables from within the company or from an outside source. A make-or-buy analysis should examine this issue from three perspectives:

1. **By performing direct cost comparisons.** Normally cost is the primary consideration in a make-or-buy analysis. Comparing costs should be fairly straightforward and the calculations should be relatively routine.
2. **By considering critical factors.** There are many factors beyond simple dollars and cents, such as attributes of the group providing deliverables, such as cost, delivery, quality, reliability, and so forth. These factors can be included in a weighted factor scoring matrix. This approach may include any number of different factors
3. **By applying appropriate filters or constraints.** Certain conditions might exist that would eliminate a given choice—make or buy—even if that choice is feasible and/or cost-effective. Here are some examples of filters or constraints (some might call them "show stoppers"):
   • Specific legal concerns
   • A need for confidentiality
   • The need or desire to maintain direct control
   • Significant excess capacity currently in your organization
   • Outsourcing the function generally unadvisable

Fourth, Formally Launch the Project

OK, let's review. We've identified the true need, determined the best way to satisfy that need, described how we're going to carry out the solution, and developed a sense of how much the solution will cost, how long it will take to carry it out, and who will be working on it. At this point, some sort of formal authorization and/or funding approval may be required before the project can proceed.

Making a Proposal for Management Approval

As a project manager, you'll have to present proposals or recommendations to management quite frequently. One of your first opportunities to make a formal proposal is likely to be at this point, after you've reviewed the requirements, identified alternative solutions, and selected a solution using financial and non-financial criteria.

I'd recommend using the format below when making any proposal to management. It may not be necessary to include all of this information in your presentation; however, fully developing each area in advance may make the process go smoother and put you in a position to answer questions that may arise during your presentation.

- **Needs Statement**—a brief description of the need
- **Background**—a more detailed description of the need, how it developed, and why it's important
- **Recommended action**—a description of the proposed project initiative or activities that would appropriately address the need, including a description of other alternatives considered and why they were rejected
- **Benefit**—a narrative description of all benefits associated with taking the proposed action
- **Action risk**—any negative impacts associated with taking the proposed action
- **Inaction risk**—any negative impacts associated with not taking the proposed action
- **Costs**—an estimate of the range (minimum, maximum, and most likely figure) of anticipated expenditures if the proposed action is taken
- **Cost savings**—an estimate of the range (minimum, maximum, and most likely figure) of the dollar savings to be achieved if the proposed action is taken
- **Schedule**—an estimate of the range (minimum, maximum, and most likely figure) of calendar time for fully implementing the recommended solution
- **Metrics**—a description of how the quality of the results

will be measured and a description of what is to be measured, monitored, or tracked while the recommendation is being implemented

- **Unknowns and uncertainties**—missing information regarding the issue and actions that could negatively affect the outcome
- **Assumptions**—a description of what took the place of the missing information
- **Constraints**—anything that limits or precludes successful implementation of the recommendation
- **Required support**—the resources needed for the proposed action
- **Liaison**—list of other organizations or people that must be involved for successful implementation, with a description of what's expected of each of them
- **Impact on others**—a description of the impact of the proposed action on other organizations, on specific individuals, on other programs or activities
- **Sponsorship**—the level of active and visible support by management or specific individuals necessary to ensure success in achieving the stated benefits
- **Critical success factors**—any issues that could make or break the project and a statement of what's required to minimize or eliminate any threats

Securing Authorization to Proceed

As stated previously, you may need to secure formal management authorization at this point to proceed with the project. In some organizations, this formal authorization comes in the form of a document called the Project Charter.

Project Charters vary widely in their design; however, many have these characteristics:

- a description of the project and its stated objectives
- anticipated team membership
- the level of authority to be granted to the project manager

- anticipated project outcomes
- customers and stakeholders
- preliminary planning information
- formal management signatures.

If your organization does not currently use a Project Charter, you may wish to create one of your own.

Conducting a Team Kickoff Meeting

In addition to following the organizational procedures described above to launch your project, you should also conduct team-oriented activities. Among the most valuable and common of these activities is the project team kickoff meeting. The formal kickoff meeting is intended to recognize the "official" formation of the team and the initiation of project execution. The timing for this event will depend upon when your team members are assigned and when you are perceived as having a "full team." Kickoff meetings can be used at a convenient time to review (or develop) mutual expectations, energize the team through presentations by members of management, and rapidly promote team cohesion.

The Unspoken Imperative: Evaluate the Political Environment

The process outlined above includes most of the formal procedures required to get your project started. If you're a savvy project manager, however, you're also sizing up the political climate that surrounds your project. Here are the basics:

Consider the potential effects for your stakeholders. Once you've identified all of your project's stakeholders, you should take that process one step further and identify who stands to gain (or lose) if your project succeeds and who will gain (or lose) if your project is deemed unsuccessful. It can be of value to understand and appreciate the nature of everyone's stake in your project.

Identify whose support will be needed. Try to identify who's in the best position to help and support your project.

Identify who is likely to work against you. Identify the parties who may feel threatened by your project or who, for whatever reason, would not like your project to succeed.

Secure a project sponsor. Identify someone in management who can serve as a sponsor for your project. Sponsors are typically members of management who have a significant amount at stake in the success or failure of your project. Sponsors can work through political issues that are beyond your sphere of influence.

Address unrealistic targets or constraints. If your proposed project targets, specifically schedule and cost, exceed management expectations, you may be forced into a situation where you're pressured into accepting cost, schedule, or other targets that are unrealistic. If this happens, I'd urge you to pursue either or both of these options:

1. *Respond with a data-driven analysis* that suggests that the project targets are unrealistic. This may or may not work, but it's certainly worth a shot.
2. *Continue to publish documents that display your original cost and schedule targets.* Once you publish documents with unrealistic targets, you've pretty much sealed your fate and doomed yourself to project failure.

Project Manager's Checklist for Chapter 4

❑ Identifying the customer's true need—the most fundamental problem or opportunity—is the first and most important step in the entire project process.

❑ Using financial criteria is the preferred method for determining whether projects are worth doing. After all, when you boil it down, projects are really financial investments. However, non-financial criteria can be used when financial information is unavailable or expensive to obtain.

❏ Using a combination of financial and non-financial criteria is an excellent way to ensure a comprehensive analysis of a prospective project opportunity. Doing this allows for consideration of the intangibles, which many people seem to like.

❏ Two key documents in defining projects are the Project Requirements Document and the Project Definition Document. The Requirements Documents details the problem or need; the Project Definition Document details the solution.

❏ Conducting a formal project "Kickoff Meeting" is an excellent way to signal everyone that the project is officially underway, and provides a head start in promoting team cohesion.

❏ Be sure to size up the political climate within your organization. Consider whether any political or cultural issues are likely to impact you or your project.

Building and Maintaining an Effective Team

ortunately, Brad decides to act upon his suspicions—and the information and insights he uncovered in his brief conversations with Bill, the Operations representative, and Ann, the engineer responsible for installing the production lines four years ago. With some investigation, some effort, and the support of several people around the company, Brad determines that there's an excellent chance that the output of the four existing lines could be increased to 800 units per week.

His proposal is overwhelmingly approved after he demonstrates how this solution is better than the one given to him. In addition to providing greater output than the original solution, it would cost considerably less! Although it took a little digging, cost a little time, and got him involved in a couple of testy conversations, Brad realizes that it was worth it.

But just as Brad is settling into his new role as corporate hero, it occurs to him that he needed the support of many people just to get his project pulled together, presented to management, and approved. The support he'd gotten from these people made him appreciate that he probably wouldn't get very far into planning and implementation without the help of those people¯and probably more. All at once, it hits him: now that his project is off and running, it's time to form his team.

The Mechanics of Building a Team

Once again, Brad's instincts have served him well. Some project managers in Brad's situation are tempted to immediately start moving forward on their own. They try to advance the project as far and as fast as possible, seeking the support of individuals only when they can't go any further. As we'll soon see, this approach may offer the promise of a quick start and appear to save money, but it's probably not a sound long-term strategy.

When Should You Form Your Team?

This is a very difficult question to answer. Conditions are rarely favorable for the "big bang" approach that some envision, where the entire team is formed at one time. The fact is that it often requires two or three iterations of soliciting team members before the team is fully formed. Very small projects may be the exception to this, however. As with many aspects of project management, the answer that's right for you will depend upon the careful balancing of several competing issues. As for deciding when to form your team, here are some considerations:

The project should be defined well enough to determine the appropriate participants. Your ability to begin the team formation process will depend upon how much effort you put into the project definition process outlined in Chapter 4. If you followed all the steps in detail, you have a great start. As a matter of fact, many of the people who helped you during project definition may very well become formal team members, once your project is formally authorized to proceed. In this case, you've already begun forming your team. However, if you did only a limited amount of work in defining the project or tried to do it solo, you have to further define the project and/or work with a small group of known participants to determine the other players, before you can begin forming your team.

The project should not be defined in so much detail that it discourages ownership. Confusing, huh? This is part of the balancing act referred to above. One of the truisms of project management (actually, this is just human nature) is that the less a person participates in the definition and planning of a project, the less likely he or she is to take "ownership" of it. So, it's not a good idea for you to define and plan the project work alone, then simply hand it to team members to implement. They'll feel that they're executing *your* plan, not theirs, and performance is likely to suffer.

Consider the expense of involvement vs. anticipated contribution. Formally assigning an individual to your project is a little bit like a hiring process. In the eyes of the organization, it authorizes that individual to begin charging his or her time (or some portion of it) to your project. If you're in an environment where you're keeping track of costs, you must immediately begin tracking the expense of the time involvement. Regrettably, this can become somewhat of a cat-and-mouse game at times.

Consider Internal Consulting

Smart Managing

Most of us tend to think of people as being either "on" or "off" a project, referring to whether they've been formally assigned. However, in the early stages of a project, getting people formally assigned to work on your project is an iffy proposition, for at least two reasons. First, the prevailing mindset is often to "keep the cost down until we figure out whether we have a project or not." If you're keeping track of hours or costs, having several people formally assigned (and therefore charging their time) to your project can be contrary to the goal of keeping investigation costs down. Second, getting people formally assigned to projects that aren't yet a sure thing can be quite challenging. Consider internal consulting as a potential alternative to formal assignment. Negotiate directly with appropriate subject matter experts or prospective team members. Agree upon a deliverable (or a level of participation) and agree upon a cost (the number of hours to be charged to your project).

Who Should Be on Your Team?

The answer to this question depends on the size and complexity of your project.

Medium and large projects in most functional organizations tend to rely on the *core team* concept. These kinds of projects often require a substantial amount of work to be performed by several functional areas (departments) within the organization. In the core team model, you try to obtain one representative from each functional area assigned to your project. This representative serves as your *single point of accountability* for all work performed within his or her department or work group.

On smaller projects, it makes more sense to examine the major elements of work to be done. You should then try to obtain individual team members according to how well their particular skills match a given element of work.

> **Key Term**
>
> **Functional manager** The boss of any member of your team. Also known as a functional supervisor, this person typically leads a specific work group, such as Marketing, Software Development, or Engineering. In most matrix organizations, functional managers are responsible for assigning the required resources to your project.

Whatever the size of your project or anticipated team configuration, it's likely that functional managers (department heads) will be viewed as the resource providers.

Ordinarily, you would seek out a given functional manager armed with information on the project and a description of the type of resource needed. In many cases, you'll probably have a specific person in mind for the assignment.

In an ideal world, the resource assigned to work on your project represents the optimum match of your needs and their skills. Unfortunately, it doesn't always work out that way.

All too often, you'll get somebody who happens to be available at the time. To be blunt, you may get offered a person who tends to be less in demand, often due to inferior skills or an undesirable behavior pattern. In other words, *everyone* wants the best resources; that's why they're often over-loaded and generally unavailable.

If you sense that this could happen, you may want to modify your approach strategy. Try to establish a climate or tone in which the functional manager, rather than the individual assigned to your project, will be viewed as being responsible for the success of that department's contribution to the project. If resource providers feel this responsibility, they should be more likely to provide a more qualified employee for your project—and pay more attention throughout the life of your project.

> **Getting the Resource You Want, Part I** TRICKS OF THE TRADE
>
> If you have a specific resource in mind, be prepared to "fight." Prepare a strong argument—in advance—to explain why you need that particular individual. Be sure that there's a *compelling functional basis* for your argument. Simply saying, "I like working with Sally" or "Joe and I get along very well" is unlikely to sway the resource provider.

In all of the above scenarios, we've assumed that you'll be using people who work within your organization. However, at times it may be necessary to use external resources. The expertise you need may not exist within your company, internal resources may not be available when you need them, or it may just make good sense to look outside. (Refer back to Chapter 4 for additional discussion on this topic.) Before using external resources, be sure to consider these additional points:

1. A competitive bidding process may be required. Selecting a qualified consultant or contractor may be tricky.
2. You'll need to write and maintain con-tracts.
3. Some flexibility may be lost (e.g., what

> **Getting the Resource You Want, Part II** TRICKS OF THE TRADE
>
> If you have a specific resource in mind, you'll need to make that very clear as soon as possible—definitely before a specific individual has been named. Getting a functional manager to change his or her mind after mak-ing a decision on a resource assign-ment is extremely difficult.

Screening Candidates for Your Team

There's no secret recipe that will guarantee a successful project team. However, asking the following questions may help you identify those who may represent the best candidates for a given role:

1. Does the candidate have the knowledge and skill to do the job? Technical and functional skills? Problem-solving skills? Interpersonal skills?
2. Does the candidate have the desired personal characteristics for the job?
3. Does the candidate believe in the goals of the project and seem likely to enthusiastically support it?
4. Does the candidate have the time to be able to devote to the project?
5. Is the candidate compatible with other team members, either already identified or under consideration?
6. Does the candidate regard participation on your project as an important function or rather as an intrusion on his or her "real job"?

---

happens if the project is cancelled or put on hold and you have a contract with an outside company?).

Identifying Who Does What

As mentioned above, individuals come on to your team with the general expectation that they represent a good "functional fit" and should be able to do the required work. It's up to you, however, to ensure that the duties you give them throughout the project reasonably match their skills. If you ask team members to stretch too far beyond their abilities, they may tend to "shut down" and difficulties will ensue. Conversely, if you grossly underutilize their talents (as least from their perspective), performance problems may also result, such as loss of interest, procrastination, and a general lack of effort.

As the project's overall scope of work becomes better defined, you can identify more specifically what each team member will do. Eventually, each person's task responsibility will be shown on a Responsibility Assignment Matrix. (We'll cover this in Chapter 7, "Preparing a Detailed Project Plan") As you move forward, it's important to allow each team member to play a major role in defining his or her specific work on the project.

In the meantime, developing an organizational chart (sometimes

> **Just Fill in the Blanks**
>
> The organizational chart or breakdown structure can be used as a template when you form the team. As you identify required functional positions, you can place the appropriate department name on the chart. Then, as specific individuals are assigned to your project, you can add their names.

known as an organizational breakdown structure) for your project team is an easy way to help everyone understand the roles and responsibilities of team members. A sample is shown in Figure 5-1.

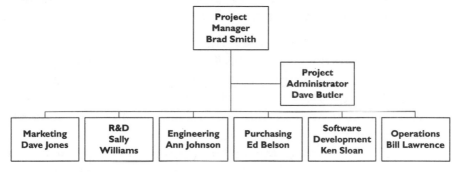

Figure 5-1. Team organization, Apex Project

Team Leadership Starts on Day One!

As Brad will soon find out, managing the project team begins immediately. From the moment that people are assigned to your project, you're responsible for ensuring that they're heading in the desired direction. This often requires significant tact and influencing ability. Since you're in a matrix organizational environment, you have no formal authority over them, so you've got to be able to lead appropriately.

Anticipating Team Members' Questions and Anxieties

One of the biggest problems that a project manager faces in the early stages of the project is managing the anxieties that can develop within the members of newly formed teams. If left unchecked, this anxiety can slow down early team growth and inhibit the development of relationships, thus affecting work output. With that in mind, let's examine some of the more common questions that you can expect to be running through their minds as you begin working with your team.

WIIFM (What's in It for me)? Once again, human nature comes to the forefront. Nearly all team members will be concerned with some form of this question. Some will wonder about the effect that participating on your project will have on their status in the organization and on their career. Others will wonder if participating on your project is likely to be personally or professionally satisfying.

What will be expected of me? This issue surfaces most often when team members are unfamiliar with your leadership style or approach. Curiously, the source of this anxiety often pertains to aspects of the role that have little to do with their required work. Team members tend to be more concerned with issues such as the amount of personal freedom they'll have, how much you'll micromanage them, or the extent of administrative, clerical, and other undesirable duties you'll expect them to perform.

What will life on your team be like? People will naturally want to know who else will be on the team and the likelihood that their relationships with other team members will be harmonious. They'll also have questions about the composition of the team. Will the team unify? Or will members constantly bicker? Will everyone on the team be qualified? Or will there be some members who will have to be "helped along"? Will all members be peers? Or will there be a hierarchy? Some of the most dysfunctional teams that people have told me about have occurred when a manager attempts to be a part of the team. Inevitably, rank surfaces as an issue—directly or indirectly.

Addressing Team Members' Questions and Anxieties

Generally speaking, you can reduce or eliminate many of these anxieties by having a conversation with your team. Specifically, consider conducting a *team meeting* as early as possible to cover the following openly and honestly:

1. Review the project objectives (the true need) and justification for doing the project (benefit to the organization).
2. Review the project proposal (the solution) and why that represents the preferred approach
3. Bring up any problems or constraints they may encounter as a team.
4. Clearly define the role of all team members in terms of their functional contribution. (Consider using the organizational breakdown structure.)
5. Try to honestly characterize your leadership style (free and open, trusting, exacting, etc.).
6. Describe your expectations regarding project logistics (frequency and timing of team meetings, for example).
7. Describe your expectations in terms of behaviors, such as team meeting conduct or preferred methods of communication.

In addition, you may want to meet individually with each member of your team, to discuss the following aspects of their involvement on the project:

1. The reason why they were selected
2. Any unique expectations you may have of them
3. Any problems or constraints they may encounter
4. What effects successful performance may have on them (*Watch out!* This one may be tricky.)

How Teams Evolve and Develop over Time

There are various models that describe how teams evolve throughout the life of a project. One of the more popular ones suggests that teams pass through four distinct "stages."

Forming: In this stage, people are gathering information about the project. They're concerned with what they'll have to do, who's on the team, how they'll fit in with the others, how your leadership style will affect them, and many other issues related to starting a project.

Storming: In this stage, team members react to what they've learned during the forming stage. They decide how much they like the project objectives, their roles and responsibilities, and the demands you've placed on them. Incidentally, they're also deciding how much they like *you* and your leadership style.

Norming: If any conflicts that arise during the storming stage are handled properly, the team will advance to the norming stage. Here, team members become reconciled with the project and their role within it. They begin to focus much more on the work to be done. Behavioral norms are developed and team members begin to know what they can expect from others.

Performing: In this stage, work becomes nearly routine. Team members work well together and produce high-quality results. All members understand one another's task responsibilities and behavioral patterns. They solve problems, make decisions, and communicate relatively smoothly.

Adjusting Your Team Leadership Style over Time

As the team evolves, so should your leadership style. Flexibility is one of the most valuable assets you can possess. The concept of flexible leadership works for both teams and individuals, as we'll see later in this chapter. Here's how the models

---

Beware of the Fifth Stage!

Smart Managing   Some have enhanced the popular model above by adding a fifth stage—Mourning. From my experience, you should expect the team's output to begin to falter. Some team members have disappeared after completing their work; those who remain may become preoccupied with "life after this project." Team members (or those remaining) scramble to complete the last few tasks, which may not have been included in the original plan. This is a difficult time for the project manager.

> ### Don't Be a Task Master
> **⚠ CAUTION!**
>
> During the forming stage, some project managers are anxious to get off to a good start by having everyone "roll up their sleeves and get to work." This approach can be dangerous—especially for teams that may need to work together for an extended period of time—since it ignores the social aspects of team evolution. Some people need time to get to know one another and become comfortable interacting. If you don't provide this opportunity, communication may be stifled, thus decreasing the team's effectiveness.

suggest adjusting your style to meet the demands of each stage described above:

Forming: In this stage, your team is generally looking to you to provide information, organization, structure, and context. Accordingly, you adopt more of a structuring/directing style. Make sure everyone understands the project, your expectations of them, the procedures to be followed, and so forth.

Storming: Conflicts tend to be greatest in the storming stage. You cannot direct the team through this period and you cannot ignore the conflict as it surfaces. To do so would threaten your ability to lead your team into the next stage and you may remain mired in conflict. A guiding/coaching style is best during this stage, as you take the necessary time to address the team's questions, concerns, and sometimes their challenges of your course of action. Be sure to explain your decisions during this difficult period.

Norming: In the norming stage, your direct involvement begins to diminish considerably as team members chart their course by laying out their work. You should encourage them to participate more actively as you adopt more of a supporting/encouraging style. Get them to take ownership for their part of the project. Without this feeling of ownership, it may be difficult to advance to the next stage.

Performing: This is a great stage for you as project manager. Your role becomes less stressful. You assign basic responsibilities and let team members play a leading role in determining the best way to carry them out. You may allow them considerable authority in decision-making as you assume a delegating/facilitating style. In this stage, you're primarily an enabler. Confident in your team's abilities, you'll tend to manage by exception, concerning yourself primarily with variances from the intended course of the project.

Mourning: In this stage, much of your project's original structure has disappeared or become irrelevant. As your team members struggle to figure out what they need to do to conclude the project successfully, you should return to the structuring/directing style of the forming stage. Organize the remaining work, assign responsibilities, and provide specific direction so you can avoid the syndrome of the never-ending project.

Fostering Teamwork and Synergism

As project manager, you provide leadership at two levels—with the team and with individuals. Though there many similarities, each has unique considerations. We'll begin by examining some of the more important leadership issues that pertain to the team as a whole.

It Takes More than a Pizza Party or Rock Climbing to Build a Team!

Teambuilding is one of the more misunderstood principles in project management. Regrettably, many people equate teambuilding with poorly orchestrated, "voluntary" social gatherings or artificial, imposed, often hokey, events. Though some of these approaches can work, they often evoke more laughter than respect, for one reason because it's difficult to pull them off without appearing manipulative.

It's well worth noting that teambuilding can occur in various ways using a variety of methods. It's also worth correcting the misconception that teambuilding events must be done in an environment away from work or the project.

The essence of building a team is very simple: get people to spend time together so that they can know one another better.

Although you can certainly do this by taking the team out to lunch, meeting after work, or organizing a social gathering, you can also do it in ways that not only tie members together, but also tie everyone to the project. In my opinion, the strong forms of teambuilding occur when the team members expand their

Team Evaluation

Consider having your team take some time out periodically to evaluate how well you're functioning as a team. This activity offers several potential benefits: it will help you address areas of concern before they grow, provide you with insights on potential areas of self-improvement, and get team members to interact outside the confines of the project tasks.

Smart Managing

knowledge of each other and the project at the same time. Here are some examples:

- Develop mutual expectations for team members and the project manager.
- Develop a project network diagram by using sticky notes on the wall.
- Develop a "code of conduct" for project team meetings.
- Celebrate significant project milestones (e.g., design approved, first unit shipped, etc.).

Recognizing and Addressing Differing Perspectives

Numerous instruments are available for characterizing personal preferences, thinking processes, communication styles, and other aspects of personality. Though the instruments differ considerably, the principle behind all of them is the same: people are different.

This rather unsurprising fact has two major implications for you as a project manager. First, individuals must be managed as individuals. (We'll explore that aspect later in this chapter.) Second, every member of your team is likely to have his or her own unique perspective on just about everything. Although this isn't news, you should continually bring it to the attention of the team. Most conflict arises from differing opinions, which are

MISTAKE PROOFING

Include Conflict Resolution Training

Because we all look at things differently, conflict among team members and between your team and you is inevitable. Conflict can lead to personality clashes and other unproductive outcomes. Be sure to include conflict resolution training as a part of your overall training and development plan. Urge others on your team to do the same.

rooted in our differing perspectives. Drawing attention to these simple realities helps team members understand that conflict is inevitable and reduces the anxiety that conflict can create. It also helps you channel conflict in a way that produces stronger, synergistic outcomes.

The Value and Purpose of Team Meetings

The most common team meeting is the regularly scheduled status review. This is where you're likely to conduct most of your *formal* project business. However, regular team meetings have other purposes beyond the obvious technical and logistical ones. They serve to continually remind your team members that they're not working alone and they must rely on one another. Team meetings also serve as the primary forum for what I call "the growth of the collective team intelligence." At each team meeting, everyone on your team learns a little bit more about the project and each other's contribution to the project.

This is one of the more underrated benefits of team meetings and it's worth specific mention. Sooner or later, some members of your team will ask to be excused from team meetings. The typical reason will be that they "don't have much going on right now." In deciding whether to release them or not, you'll have to weigh the value of their presence (in terms of the growth of the collective intelligence) against their perception that you're wasting their time. It might be more appropriate to consider the extent to which their absence may affect team cohesion and synergy.

Managing Team Interaction

Fledgling project managers often make the mistake of assum-

Smart
Managing

Conducting Effective Team Meetings

One of the primary reasons why people dislike team meetings is because they're conducted very poorly. Here are a few simple rules:

1. Publish a meeting notice in advance, with agenda items and anticipated time allocations.
2. Start and finish the meeting on time.
3. Don't repeat everything for latecomers.
4. Release everyone as soon as business has been conducted.
5. Cancel a meeting if you believe there's nothing new to discuss.
6. Limit the meeting to project management issues; don't let it be a forum for a few members to hash out detailed design decisions.
7. Publish brief meeting notes that emphasize action items; highlight those due by the next meeting.

ing that their primary role is to direct the day-to-day actions of team members. This approach is guaranteed to enrage experienced team members. It also overlooks a key aspect of team leadership. *One of your most important responsibilities is interface management.* You're the only person in the organization responsible for ensuring a healthy working relationship between and among the members of the project team. And it's unlikely that all of the desired interactions will take place without some help from you. Your role in fostering teamwork and synergism may require you to devote some energy to "designing and engineering" the interaction between team members.

You should encourage team members to interact *whenever the need arises*. Discourage them from waiting until the next team meeting to address any issues or concerns they may have with each other. Waiting wastes time and opportunities. However, you also need to know what's going on, so make sure that team members keep you informed whenever they take important actions or make important decisions.

What About Rewards and Recognition?

This is one of the most difficult aspects of a project manager's job. I include this topic under fostering teamwork, which reflects my personal bias. Although philosophies and approaches to rewards and recognition vary widely, I'd urge you to consider two simple points relative to this important topic.

Rewarding teams reinforces the team concept. Some organizations promote teamwork, but reward and recognize individual performance. This sends a mixed message and can undermine teamwork. If you reward and recognize teams and teamwork, the greatest contributors may feel slighted, but it's still the best way to show that you value teamwork. Your projects are more likely to succeed when your team members work together to succeed as a team.

Rewarding individual heroics promotes undesirable behavior. Quipsters often say that "rewarding firefighting only serves to promote arson." Funny, but true. When organizations (or project managers) develop a reputation for rewarding the individual hero who rides in on the white horse to save the day, they risk setting up an environment that's counterproductive to teaming. Even worse, they may be encouraging some individuals to undermine the efforts of their teammates as a way to inflate their own importance.

Getting the Most from Individual Team Members

In the previous section, we examined several aspects of managing the project team as a unit. Savvy project managers recognize that team leadership also involves effectively managing one-on-one relationships. You must manage both the team and individual members simultaneously and with equal care and consideration. Let's examine some of the key aspects of managing the individual team members.

What People Need to Do Their Job

You can't expect your team members to effectively carry out their duties unless they have certain basics. Although interpretations vary, most models of individual performance include some form of the following basics:

1. A clearly stated objective (for the entire project and for specific tasks)
2. The purpose (value or benefit) of achieving the objective
3. Direction and guidance for achieving the objective (plans and processes)
4. The skills required to do the job
5. The tools and resources required to do the job
6. Feedback on their performance
7. A description of their limits of authority
8. A desire to perform

As the project manager, you can address all of these conditions, with the possible exception of #8. You should strive to ensure that each team member has these basics throughout the life of the project. You may have to be proactive. You cannot always rely upon team members to bring deficiencies to your attention. In some cases, they may not even be aware of their own deficiencies.

Establishing Mutual Expectations

Earlier in this chapter, we examined the purpose and value of meeting individually with each member of your team. One of the most productive and powerful things you can do in these meetings is to establish a set of mutual expectations between you and the individual member. This will help solidify and clarify your working relationship. Some of the more common expectations are listed in Figure 5-2.

The expectations listed in Figure 5-2 are generic. You'll probably want to expand this list to include expectations specific to your project, your particular situation, and each individual team member.

Informal Leadership

As mentioned in Chapter 2, an informal network often exists within an organization as a kind of "subculture." A similar phenomenon exists at the project level. Although it's true that much of the project business is conducted through formal methods such as

Project Managers Expect Team Members to:	Team Members Expect the Project Manager to:
• Be committed to the project	• Stimulate group interaction
• Provide accurate and truthful status	• Promote participative planning
• Follow the project plan and defined processes	• Define all relevant work processes
• Demonstrate proactivity	• Define performance expectations
• Take direction, but push back appropriately	• Manage conflict in a constructive manner
• Propose things that make sense	• Share information appropriately
• Communicate / inform proactively	• Remove obstacles
• Be accountable for decisions	• Insulate team from unproductive pressures
• Be respectful of other team members	• Resist unnecessary changes
• Maintain a positive attitude	• Recognize and reward achievement

Figure 5-2. Developing mutual expectations

team meetings, savvy project managers recognize that more important business is often conducted through informal means.

It can be beneficial to visit team members in their workplace occasionally or to call team members from time to time "just to see how it's going." It'll help you maintain good relationships, show your interest, and offer an avenue of information that may help you run the project more effectively.

One caution: you must do it for the right reasons, in good faith, and primarily in order to manage the project better. If you chat just to get one team member to tell you about another, for example, the strategy will quickly backfire. Also, if your interest in team members is not sincere, it will probably show.

Note: All Team Members Are Not Created Equal

One of the best methods for getting the most from individual team members is to simply treat them as individuals. There are several models that attempt to describe the principle of flexible leadership by using factors such as the work to be done vs. the readiness of the individual to successfully perform the work. These models use this kind of analysis to yield a recommended leadership style for a given individual. The styles that most mod-

els ultimately suggest are
similar to the team leadership styles described above
(structuring, guiding, supporting, delegating).

I would encourage you
to individualize the principle of flexible leadership
even more. Recognize that
people have individual
needs that you can't meet

> **Honesty Is the
> Best Policy**
> **Smart Managing**
>
> Meeting informally one on
> one with individual team members
> provides opportunities to discuss
> issues openly and frankly. To get accu-
> rate and reliable input, you must
> establish an environment where team
> members can speak freely and hon-
> estly during these sessions.

simply with one of four styles. Be aware, however, that truly
managing individuals as individuals requires courage, insight,
and intelligence. You'll need to determine what motivates each
individual on your team, then provide it whenever you can and
whenever it makes sense to do so, but in ways that don't show
favoritism.

Even if you do, however, sometimes some people will want
to know why you're treating someone differently. You'll need to
have a reasonable and fair-handed explanation.

I once worked for a person who had this ability. As a result,
the people in his work group would consistently give their all.
Why? Because they felt he truly cared about them as individuals—and they didn't want to let him down.

Project Manager's Checklist for Chapter 5

❑ Despite the popular vision that the team magically comes
together at one time and begins work, the reality is that
team members will slowly trickle onto your team as you
realize your needs.

❑ You should err on the side of getting members assigned as
soon as you can, rather than "until there's more definition."
Their participation in defining the project is likely to reap
benefits in the form of higher commitment to the success
of the project.

❏ If there's a specific person you want on your team, prepare an argument as to why you need that person. Make sure you put your request in before the assignment is made—resource providers aren't ordinarily inclined to reverse a decision, once they've made it.

❏ Don't be afraid to "screen" candidates who have been assigned to your project. Confirm that their qualifications, attitude, and track record qualify them to do the job. If you have concerns, voice them early and factually.

❏ Members of newly formed teams will have questions, concerns, and anxieties. You should address these issues early in the project, before they turn into problems. Conduct an open team meeting and review the project, your expectations, and your project leadership philosophy. This is likely to answer many of their questions or concerns.

❏ As the team evolves and matures, they will tend to become more and more "self-sufficient," requiring less direct involvement on your part. You should adjust your leadership style over the course of the project according to their rate of growth.

❏ Good team leadership recognizes that everyone is different. This suggests that trying to manage everyone on the team exactly the same way is flawed thinking. Don't be afraid to manage individuals as individuals.

An Overview of Planning and Estimating

It's often been said that project management really consists of two *major* phases—doing the right project and doing the project right. Ensuring that your project is based upon a true need and that it's justified from a business standpoint are two important aspects of *doing the right project.* Project planning, on the other hand, is all about *doing the project right.*

Project planning gets more attention than any other aspect of project management—and justifiably so. It's hard to imagine how a project could be successful without some planning.

In addition to being important, project planning is also an *enormous* subject. I often think of it as consisting of two components. The first is almost strategic; it consists of understanding some of the *principles and philosophies* of planning. The second component of project planning is tactical—almost *mechanical;* it consists of the step-by-step process of creating a detailed project plan, using estimates as raw material.

Brad will soon realize that he's transitioning from doing the right project to doing the project right. He'll need to prepare estimates and create a detailed plan for making sure that he does Project Apex right.

Before we rejoin Brad in this endeavor, let's take a closer look at some of those principles and philosophies of planning—and of estimating.

An Introduction to Project Planning

As much as we talk about project planning, it's an elusive thing to characterize in a few words or graphics. Why? Well, for one thing, "the plan" can assume many different shapes, sizes, and forms. Many people equate the *plan* with the *schedule*, but. as we'll see, there's much more to a plan than just a schedule.

Project plans are considered to consist of three fundamental "dimensions"

- cost: how much money that will be spent and how it's budgeted over time
- time: how long it will take to execute work—individually and as a total project
- scope: what is to be done

Creating an accurate, credible project plan requires a

Scope—A Tale of Two Meanings

Smart Managing   The term *scope* actually has two meanings that are quite different in concept. It's important to understand what each meaning represents and how they are applied in discussions you may have.

Project scope is a term that's most closely associated with the mission, goals, and objectives of the project. It may be thought of as the overall size of the project or a high-level description of what the project will tackle. For example, building and installing a few storage racks has a much smaller *project scope* than installing a computer-controlled storage and retrieval system.

Scope of work refers to all of the individual elements of work (taken collectively) that must be performed to accomplish the project. The efforts represented by all of the items that appear on your schedule or in your activities listing constitute the *scope of work*.

significant amount of effort and the input of many people. Attempting to create a project plan single-handedly has caused the downfall of more than one project manager. In essence, the project plan is a kind of map that you can use to guide you and your team from beginning to end.

One reason that planning is so difficult to describe definitively is because *project plans are always evolving.* The instant Brad transitions from asking, "What are we trying to accomplish?" (the true need) to asking, "How are we going to accomplish it?" (the project definition), the process of planning begins. And although he may not appreciate it right now, Brad will be continuing that process until the very end of Project Apex.

Organizations vary considerably in their general approach to project planning. The specific procedures that your organization prescribes reflects its philosophy toward planning and control. If your organizational management tends to be extremely action-oriented or to not believe in the value of planning, it's likely that your planning procedures will be minimal. In this environment, projects may be hastily initiated and a significant amount of upfront planning is done without much thought or without properly considering alternatives or risks. Conversely, if your organizational management has a bias toward certainty or control, that's likely to be reflected in the development and use of rigorous planning procedures.

The Planning Process

As mentioned above, project plans tend to emerge gradually. They are continuously modified and refined in terms of content, structure, and level of detail. As the project definition becomes more refined, work is broken down into ever-increasing levels of detail, assumptions are verified or refuted, and actual results are achieved, the project plan must keep pace.

Although there are many variations of the basic project planning process, Figure 6-1 illustrates a common phenomenon. Project plans are often generated in iterations: at different times, in different levels of detail, for different purposes. Major

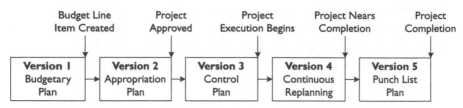

Figure 6-1. The evolution of project plans

iterations are often tied to key decision points and result in the creation of different versions of the plan at different levels of detail and precision.

As Figure 6-1 shows, the first version of the project plan occurs before the project (as most people know it) has been defined. In this version, estimates of cost and schedule are relatively crude and are established with little knowledge of the specifics of the project. It's done primarily for the purpose of allocating funds to an effort that will be listed in an organization's annual operating budget.

The next version of the project plan is created when the organization is prepared to initiate a project represented in its operating budget. Sufficient planning must be done so that it can be formally decided whether or not the project is an investment worth funding. (Chapter 4 dealt extensively with this *initiation phase* of the project.)

If the project proposal is approved, the next version of the plan emerges. A detailed plan is created that the project team will use as a guide for implementation and that you will use to evaluate progress and maintain control. Many of the planning tools and techniques used during this stage of the project are covered in this chapter.

I like to refer to the next stage in the evolution of the project plan as *continuous replanning*. As the team executes the project, change will occur. Actual results will inevitably be different from what was expected at the outset of the project, so you'll need to make ongoing course adjustments. These continual changes should be reflected in slight modifications to the plan.

The last version of the plan is not covered in most books on project management, but I've found it to be quite real and very vital to achieving success. It occurs near the end of the project, when it becomes apparent that a number of work items (sometimes referred to as a *punch list*) must be taken care of in order for the project to be considered complete. When you reach this stage, you may find it useful to create a new plan, just for completing all remaining work. This allows for a highly focused and efficient effort and will help you avoid being associated with a legendary "project that never ends."

> **⚠ CAUTION!**
>
> **Planning Is Not a One-Time Event!**
> It's inevitable that conditions will change during your project: someone may be pulled off your team, resources may become unavailable when you need them, the business climate may shift, material shortages could occur, and so forth. As conditions change, your original plan must be modified to reflect those changes. The *project plan is a living document* and you should expect to be planning throughout the life of your project.

Beware! Common Planning Failures

Before diving into the details of creating project plans, it might be worthwhile to look at some of the common mistakes that some project managers make in their approach to planning. This will not only help you to avoid them, but also provide valuable background for what we'll cover in this chapter and the next.

Failure to Plan. As we'll soon see, many factors influence the degree to which you should plan your project. Sometimes, a relatively small amount of planning effort will suffice. However, some project managers feel (or are pressured into feeling) that planning is not worth doing at all. Some project managers—particularly new ones—are extremely action-oriented. They feel that time spent in planning is lost. Others are pressured by their management, their organizational culture, or some stakeholders into cutting short any meaningful planning effort. To those groups, when people are sitting around planning, it simply doesn't seem that progress is being made. However, project managers who don't plan chronically suffer from an interesting irony. Because they don't plan, they spend a great deal of time "fighting fires," so they're always going full speed. Since they're going at full speed, they're able to rationalize their negligence in planning because they're too busy and don't have the time. Don't let this be you!

Failure to Plan in Sufficient Detail. Sometimes project managers make an attempt to plan, but don't do it in enough detail. It's a question of how they size and compose elements of work—specifically the ones that they then put on their schedule and attempt to watch closely. Failing to plan and schedule project work in enough detail can result in three significant, undesirable effects, which you can avoid by asking these questions:

1. Will all involved participants readily understand what it includes?

    You should *describe and define* elements of work in enough detail that there's no confusion. I've seen many cases where defining work elements poorly has resulted in rework, as people simply misunderstood what was expected. For example, let's assume Brad's project contains an element of work entitled "analyze existing production lines." Brad may think that he knows what this element entails. It certainly seems like something he or a member of his team should do. However, think about it for a moment: would you be able to make an intelligent guess as to exactly what's included in this element? It's simply not defined in sufficient detail to make it unambiguous to all concerned. This element of work is too big; it should be broken down.

2. Can you prepare a reasonably accurate estimate of duration and cost?

    If a reasonably accurate estimate is needed, the work must be broken down to a point where you can estimate its duration and cost with a high degree of confidence. In other words, the less time and effort you put into defining your project, the greater the uncertainty in your estimate. We'll discuss this point in more detail later in this chapter.

Size Them Right!

There are two rules of thumb regarding how far to break down the work on a project, to determine what elements of work you'll put on your schedule and track. Both of these rules are reasonable and valid.

One popular rule of thumb suggests that you should size schedule items at around 40-80 labor hours.

The second rule—and the one I recommend—suggests that you try to size schedule items proportional to the project—at around 4% of overall project duration. For example, if a project will take only six months, schedule items should be about one week in duration. For an 18-month long project, three weeks is probably a reasonable size. Remember, these are guidelines only.

3. Will you be able to effectively monitor its progress?

The principle is quite simple. To make sure that your project is staying on schedule, you'll need to be able to gauge that team members are making progress as expected. The most convenient way to gauge their progress is by observing the completion of relatively small elements of work routinely—typically at your project team meetings. Therefore, elements of work need to be broken down enough that you can verify their completion readily.

Failure to Know When to Stop Planning. This can be just as much a problem as not planning in enough detail. Some people believe that the further they break down the work, the more control they'll achieve. That's simply not true.

Let's say that you're managing a 14-month project and you conduct team status meetings every two weeks. If you plan in such detail that your elements of work are only a few days in duration, several of them may (or may not!) be completed *between team meetings*. So, you won't benefit from the greater planning unless you check on progress almost daily. If you just depend on status reports every two weeks, many of your schedule details probably won't matter.

In addition, if your work elements are sized too small, creating the schedule and keeping it up to date could become an

MISTAKE PROOFING

Synchronization Is the Key

The frequency of your team meetings and the size of the work elements on your schedule should be approximately proportionate. This provides a reasonable balance between your need to maintain control and the amount of effort required to create and maintain your schedule. The 4% rule of thumb provides a good guideline for scheduling meetings as well as for sizing work elements.

administrative nightmare. The paperwork involved will not endear you to your team, either!

Failure to Involve Task Performers in Planning. This mistake has been mentioned a couple of times already, but it's worth repeating. The principle is simple: the people who will be working on your project should be heavily involved in planning their portion of it. There are at least two good reasons for this. First, the planning outputs will undoubtedly be more accurate as the task performers are probably more knowledgeable than you—after all, it's what they do. Second, involving them during the planning stage is likely to make them significantly more willing to participate and more committed to succeeding. People often feel compelled to live up to what they've promised.

Failure to Reflect Risk and Uncertainty in Plans. Chapter 8 is entirely dedicated to the subjects of risk and uncertainty. Why? Because it's a very big deal. Nearly all projects that go awry do so because risk and uncertainty were left untreated. *Risk management techniques use statistics and other scientific methods to allow you to make the most reasonable prediction of an outcome in conditions of high uncertainty.* Yet many who plan projects do not properly assess, accommodate, or plan for the inherent risk in projects. There are at least three reasons why this happens:

- *Project managers don't understand risk management.* Although risk management techniques have been available for quite some time, many project managers still don't know how to properly deal with risk, so they ignore it. If you're not familiar with these techniques, I'd recommend that you make the study of risk manage-ment an integral part of your self-development plans.

- *Project managers are victims of the "rose-colored glasses" syndrome.* When they prepare project plans, they tend to plan to an *all-success scenario.* They simply visualize that everything will go perfectly. Projects that are planned this way have only one direction to go—downhill.
- *Project managers yield to pressure from stakeholders, clients, or the market.* Generally speaking, risk and uncer-tainty have the *apparent* effect of extending schedules or making things cost more. That's an unfortunate perception, one that puts project managers under tremendous pressure to ignore or underplay the effects of risk. I once knew a project manager who'd taken great pains to properly assess and plan for risk on his project. Unfortunately, this extended the most likely completion date beyond the end date that had been imposed. He presented his thorough and thought-ful analysis to his management, reporting that he would not be able to complete the project in the allotted time frame with a high degree of confidence, given the current assumptions. What was the reaction from his manage-ment? "Fine. Then we'll get somebody who can!"

Failure to Keep the Plan Current. For some project managers, planning is a one-shot deal. They create a plan and then store it away in a notebook on their shelf for the remainder of the proj-ect. Project plans *must* be kept current. They must continuously reflect what's occurring on the project. Variations from the origi-nal plan are inevitable. If you don't take these variations into account, it's harder to maintain control, chaos is more likely, and you hurt your chances of bringing the project in on time and within budget.

How Much Planning Is Enough?

As is true of so many questions that arise in project manage-ment, the answer to this question is ... *it depends.* In this case, it depends upon many factors. Among the most important are the following.

Organizational Expectations. As mentioned above, organizations have different perspectives on the value of planning. This will reflect directly upon the time and effort teams are expected to put into planning. It's absolutely vital that you understand your organization's expectations relative to planning. If they're very low, I'd urge you to exceed them—to improve your chances of success. Just do it without a lot of fanfare.

Project Importance. This factor is associated more with organizational politics than technical or logistical criteria. If you're politically astute, you'll realize that there's likely to be much more attention paid to the so-called "hot project" than to other, more mundane projects. This is not to suggest that you should neglect planning for less glamorous projects—you just may be wise to put a little more into the planning and control of the high-visibility ones.

> **TRICKS OF THE TRADE**
>
> ## Discovering What Your Organization Expects
>
> It's smart to understand what your organization expects of you as a project manager—for example, how much time and effort you should put into planning. As with other types of organizational expectations, talk to your peers. Sometimes, what's in your organization's documented procedures may not accurately reflect reality. Experienced project managers have discovered that behavior (i.e., "what they do") is a more reliable indicator of expectations than documented procedures (i.e., "what they say").

Project Complexity. Projects can vary considerably in complexity. Those that require a significant amount of coordination among parties, that have intricate timing, or that include a lot of participating work groups, for example, will ordinarily require more effort and forethought in planning.

Project Size. Obviously, large projects require more planning than small ones. However, the time allocated to planning and the control of large projects can often be proportionately less.

Fitness for Use

Smart Managing

When trying to figure out how much planning is enough, keep in mind the general principle of *fitness for use*. "Fitness for use" is a term used in quality management and in business law. The application of the term to project management is very similar. In this case, however, it simply means *do what makes sense*. For example, imagine that your organization's prescribed project process has 50 steps. The fitness-for-use principle means that you should *consider* all 50 steps, but recognize that—for a variety of reasons—only 40 add value, given your project circumstances. This will save you from losing time and wasting effort mindlessly following procedures. Before skipping any steps, however, be sure that the appropriate stakeholders are aware of what you're doing, know why you're doing it, and agree with your approach.

One of the reasons this is true goes back to the point of project importance. In many organizations, mega-projects get more visibility and therefore more attention. Another reason is that smaller projects have a smaller margin of error. In other words, it doesn't take much of an incident to throw a small project well off target proportionately.

Amount of Uncertainty. When the level of uncertainty is extremely high, detailed planning of the *entire project* at the outset may not be advisable. In fact, it may be a waste of time, due to amount of change likely. On projects where the level of uncertainty is high, you'll probably end up doing the same amount of planning, but spread out periodically throughout the life of the project. In other words, expect to spend a good deal of time replanning, as you encounter change.

Project Management Software Selection. Your choice of project management software (if you use it) will affect your planning time. Obviously, the more user-friendly the software, the less time you'll have to invest in using it. However, be aware that project management software products differ significantly in cost, capability, and utility.

An Introduction to Estimating

Estimating is a big part of project planning. To prepare an accurate, thorough project plan, you'll need to estimate many things: how long it will take to do the work, how much the work will cost, how much money the project will save or make, the magnitude of the risk and uncertainty involved, and other aspects of the project. With that in mind, it's worth taking some time to discuss the process of estimating as a subset of planning.

It's Just a Guess, for Pete's Sake!

Webster defines estimating as "determining approximately the size, extent, value, cost, or nature of something." As many experienced project managers will gladly tell you, the operative word in that definition is *approximately*. The nature of project work is such that—even with significant prior experience—the uncertainty inherent in projects simply does not allow for absolute precision in estimates. Yet many people won't understand this point. And as you manage more and more projects, you will find this to be an issue with some people: they'll expect more precision and certainty in your estimates than you're able to provide. Consider this an opportunity to help them learn, to help them understand that, despite your best efforts to provide good estimates, "It's just a guess, for Pete's sake!"

Estimating Approaches

OK, so an estimate is essentially a guess. But what can you do to make it the best possible guess?

Here are five methods for obtaining estimates:

1. Ask the person responsible for doing the work to prepare the estimate.
2. Ask a subject matter expert—a person with knowledge or experience in that area.
3. Use historical data and make appropriate adjustments.
4. Use mockups, trial runs, tests, field studies, or other simulated experiences as a guide.
5. Prepare the estimate yourself.

Although all of these approaches are valid, some will work better than others. The best approach will depend upon factors such as the availability of historical data, the estimating skills of task performers or subject matter experts, and the amount of time available to prepare an estimate. You may want to try more than one approach, then use your judgment to come up with the best estimate. Remember: estimates should reflect what you believe to be the most likely outcome. Don't be afraid to apply your own judgment to the input you receive, as long as you have a rational reason to do so.

Estimating Pitfalls

Estimating is difficult. There are many things that can undermine the accuracy or validity of your estimates. Among the most common pitfalls are the following:

- **Poorly defined scope of work.** This can occur when the work is not broken down far enough or individual elements of work are misinterpreted.
- **Omissions.** Simply put, you forget something.
- **Rampant optimism.** This is the rose-colored glasses syndrome described previously, when the all-success scenario is used as the basis for the estimate.
- **Padding.** This is when the estimator (in this case almost always the task performer) includes a factor of safety *without your knowledge,* a cushion that ensures that he or she will meet or beat the estimate.
- **Failure to assess risk and uncertainty.** As mentioned earlier, neglecting or ignoring risk and uncertainty can result in estimates that are unrealistic.
- **Time pressure.** If someone comes up to you and says, "Give me a ballpark figure by the end of the day" and "Don't worry, I won't hold you to it," *look out!* This almost always spells trouble.
- **The task performer and the estimator are at two different skill levels.** Since people work at different levels of efficiency, sometimes affecting time and cost for a task

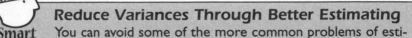

Reduce Variances Through Better Estimating

Smart Managing   You can avoid some of the more common problems of estimating by taking the following measures:

- Whenever possible, make sure that estimates are prepared by the person performing the task.
- Ask estimators to provide a basis of estimate for all estimates they submit.
- Conduct team or subject matter expert reviews of estimates.
- Resist the organizational practice of "across the board" estimate revisions (e.g., asking everyone to trim their estimates by 10%).
- During execution, promote an atmosphere that allows (if not encourages) task performers to revise estimates, as new information becomes available.

significantly, try to take into consideration who's going to do the work.

- **External pressure.** Many project managers are given specific targets of cost, schedule, quality, or performance (and often more than one!). If you're asked to meet unrealistic targets, you may not be able to fight it, but you should communicate what you believe is reasonably achievable.
- **Failure to involve task performers.** It's ironic: an estimate developed without involving the task performer could be quite accurate, but that person may not feel compelled to meet the estimate, since "it's your number, not mine," so the estimate may appear wrong.

Contingency: The Misunderstood Component

There are a number of technical definitions for *contingency*—basically, any time, money, and/or effort added to the project plan to allow for uncertainty, risk, unknowns, and errors. However, I've always found it better to describe contingency—and its proper use—in common terms and using logic. So close your eyes and imagine .... (But keep reading!)

You're at the very beginning of a project. You cannot possibly know how everything will turn out. There's just too much uncertainty and risk ahead. However, you're required to come

An Estimate Is More than Just a Number

TRICKS OF THE TRADE

We often think of an estimate as a figure alone. But if you get into the habit of making the following items part of every estimate you prepare and present, you'll be helping yourself and others to understand the true nature of estimates:

• **A range of possible outcomes.** Provide more than just your best guess (or most likely outcome). Always indicate that the final outcome *could* fall somewhere within a range. To give an exact figure without this type of qualification suggests a level of knowledge or insight that you probably don't have. The size of the range should reflect your level of uncertainty.

• **The basis for your estimate.** Describe how you calculated the estimated value and what assumptions you made in arriving at that figure. You'll also use this information as valuable insight when changes occur later on.

• **Any factors that could affect estimate validity.** Some estimates have limitations outside of which the validity of the estimate cannot be assured. For example, will your estimate be valid three months from now? Is it valid throughout the U.S., or only in the Southwest? Will it be valid if the work is subcontracted?

up with an estimate that represents your best attempt at predicting the final outcome of the project, most notably in terms of cost and schedule.

A powerful combination of your knowledge of the project, your sense of what you don't know, your experiences on previous projects, the documented experiences of countless other project managers, and some good old-fashioned project manager judgment of your own leads you to the conclusion that an estimating shortfall exists. In other words, there's a gap between the sum of your individual work element estimates and where you know you'll end up at project completion. This gap is created by your inability to understand exactly how to synthesize all of the uncertainties. According to traditional project management practices, the gap is supposed to be plugged using—you guessed it—contingency.

And now the real world . . . .

There's relentless pressure to do things faster, cheaper, and better—sometimes unrealistically so. And there's a general lack of understanding of what contingency is supposed to represent. And finally, there's the perception by some that contingency is really a slush fund for mistakes, as it's typically modeled as something tacked onto the project bottom line.

Help has arrived, however, and I'd strongly urge you to use it. There are software products that use statistics to help you calculate contingency to accommodate risk, uncertainty, and unknowns in a relatively painless manner. Although there are some slight differences, most work the same way. You provide ranges of possible outcomes for individual elements of work. The tool then simulates the execution of the project as many as one thousand times. The outputs associate a range of project outcomes correlated to various levels of confidence (confidence in your ability to meet or beat that particular outcome).

Project Manager's Checklist for Chapter 6

❑ The project plan is much more than just the schedule. It comprises many documents.

❑ Project planning is *not* a one-time event. You'll probably prepare several iterations of the project plan in increasing levels of detail, as the project is being initiated and launched. In addition, you'll be continually revising it throughout the project.

❑ Remember! There are two meanings for the term scope: *project scope* refers to the objectives of the project and *scope of work* refers to the activities to be performed.

❑ Expressing estimates in terms of ranges of outcomes, rather than precise numbers, will help others understand the uncertain nature of projects.

❑ If the length of the work elements on your schedule is about the same as your team meeting frequency, you'll optimize project control. It's reasonable to make both about 4% of the overall project length.

Preparing a Detailed Project Plan: Step by Step

B rad leans back in his chair as he finishes his turkey sandwich. Life is good. He's come a long way since that first wave of panic hit him in Susan's office, when she made him a project manager. He can recall the strange sound of the term "my project" the first few times he said it out loud. Now he actually likes the way it sounds. And why shouldn't he? He's learned a lot—and accomplished a lot—in a relatively short time.

He's learned that project management is both a science and an art—partly mechanical, partly behavioral. He believes he knows what it takes to be a good project manager and what it takes to produce a successful project outcome. He believes he already understands the project management process fairly well: he demonstrated that when he came up with a much more cost-effective solution than the one Susan had handed him.

Finally, he's proud of the way he was able to work with others in the organization (many of whom were now on his team) to prepare and present a comprehensive business case for his project. *And I got it approved by management in record time,* he thinks to himself and smiles.

Suddenly he lurches forward in his chair.

"How am I going to get all of this work done?" He picks up the inch-thick folder containing the documentation already accumulating on Project Apex. "We need to create a plan!"

Identifying What Needs to Be Done (Scope Management)

The first step in the planning process consists of identifying exactly what you're going to do, the *scope of work*. In this stage, you identify major elements of work and then break them down systematically into smaller and smaller pieces, until each piece becomes a comfortable size to estimate, execute, and monitor.

Some Basic Definitions

Here are some terms commonly used in scope management:

Activity or Task Many definitions exist for these two terms. I tend to use them interchangeably to describe an element of work. Purists might say that tasks are smaller elements of work than activities, but there's actually no standard for this. Activities consume resources. They have a finite length (time) and an expected cost.

Responsibility Assignment Matrix (RAM) The RAM is a two-axis chart that shows how the project work is assigned. It correlates specific elements of work with specific task performers.

Work Breakdown Structure (WBS) The WBS is a graphical tool—perhaps the most foundational tool in the project planning process. It organizes all of the project work by placing elements of work into logical groupings.

Work Package This term has a variety of definitions. I like to think of work packages as having two key characteristics:
- They will appear somewhere on your WBS.
- They are deliverable-oriented—that is, executing a work package typically produces some tangible or verifiable outcome.

Breaking Down the Work: The Work Breakdown Structure

Identifying and breaking down the work to be done is the logical starting point in the entire planning process. The objective of this step is to identify relatively small, specific pieces of work. (For simplicity, let's refer to them as activities.) Once you've identified all of the activities required to execute the project, you're ready to create a complete project plan. You'll be able to estimate activity durations and prepare your schedule, estimate activity costs and prepare your project budget, assign responsibility, and carry out many more planning steps.

But what exactly does a work breakdown structure look like and how do you create one?

Let's say I'm planning on hosting a birthday party in my back yard. As most people would tend to do intuitively, I begin by recognizing that there are a number of large "chunks" of work (also called subgroups) to be done. I'll have to do some planning. I'll need to make sure I properly feed everyone. I'm sure I'll need supplies of some sort, such as tables and chairs, paper plates, and so forth. I'll also have to set up for the party and clean up after the party is over. I've already begun subdividing the work to be done. Figure 7-1 shows my WBS so far.

The key at this point is to verify, as well as possible, that I've identified all major categories of work that constitute the project. In other words, *every* element of work required for my party will fit into one of these five subgroups. Since I believe this is the case, I can proceed to the next level of detail.

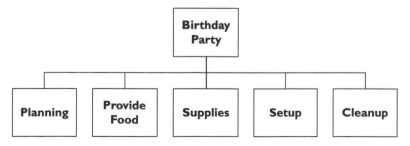

Figure 7-1. Second level of WBS for birthday party

Figure 7-2. Level 3 of WBS for setup

I begin by considering everything I'll need to do regarding Setup. I realize that I'll have to clean the pool and set up the volleyball net. I'll also have to make the yard presentable. I'll have to put up the party tent, bring out tables and chairs, and so forth. It occurs to me that there seem to be *natural groupings* of activities here, related to games and entertainment, to cleaning, and to furniture. These are the groupings that I will use for this level, as shown in Figure 7-2.

I reflect on these three categories and feel confident that everything that I have to do to set up for the party can be placed in one of these three buckets. However, I don't feel as if I've broken down the work far enough yet. *Set Up—Games and Entertainment,* for example, is just not specific enough. As I ask myself questions such as "What games?," "How much time will it take?" and "What do I have to do to pull this off?" I realize I need to go to one more level of detail. When I've eventually identified these activities, I feel confident that I know what I have to do to set up for the party (Figure 7-3).

I continue this same thought process until I've developed my entire WBS to the appropriate level of detail.

Why Create a WBS, Anyway?

So why am I suggesting that you take the time and trouble to create a work breakdown structure? Couldn't you just start list-

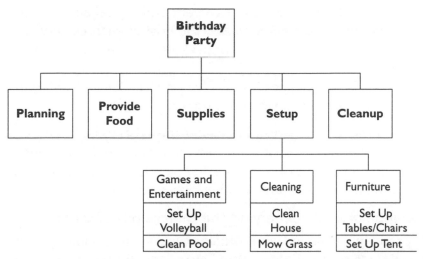

Figure 7-3. level 4 of WBS for setup

ing out activities and throw them onto a schedule? Yes, you could. However, without a frame of reference, your chances of being able to identify all of the elements of work required to execute the project are just about zero. And guess when you'd find out that something was missing—in the middle of the project.

> **Think About the Work Only**
>
> In the example of the birthday party, you may have noticed that I wasn't concerned about timing or sequence of activities as I developed my WBS. That's OK. In fact, your only concern in developing your WBS should be to thoroughly identify all work necessary to execute the project. Worrying about issues such as duration, cost, and resources will only cause confusion; address these issues later in the planning process.

There are several other good reasons why it's smart to do good WBS:

- The WBS provides an easy-to-read graphical representation of the work, allowing stakeholders to review it thoroughly for missing elements of work.
- People often underestimate the effort required to execute a project. A fully developed WBS underscores how much work there really is.

- The WBS provides a convenient and logical structure for estimating the duration and the cost of each activity, as well as for assigning responsibilities and resources to activities.
- The WBS provides an excellent source for examining the risks associated with the project.

As I mentioned earlier, I consider the WBS to be the most foundational (and perhaps the most valuable) tool in the entire project planning process. As we'll see in the next section, it provides the basis for nearly all other planning steps.

Moving Forward: Identifying the Dimensions of Work

A properly developed work breakdown structure allows you to identify every single element of work (activity) required to complete the project. Once you've done this, you're now able to move rapidly forward in the planning process.

For each of those activities, you'll now need to consider important characteristics, which I call the *dimensions*. You will use these dimensions as input for future planning steps:

- **Time:** The number of days (weeks?) that will be spent working on the activity
- **Cost:** How much will be spent on labor and materials
- **Scope:** The work that will be done, how it will be done, and what will be produced
- **Responsibility:** The person accountable for its successful completion
- **Resources:** Supporting labor, materials, or supplies needed
- **Quality:** How well the work should be done; how well any outputs should perform
- **Relationship to Other Activities:** Activities that need to be completed before this one can start

A Nifty Application of the WBS

The WBS can be a very useful tool from a graphical standpoint as well as a functional standpoint. One of techniques that I recommend to project managers is to use an extended version of the WBS as a fill-in-the-blank worksheet for capturing and displaying some of the dimensions as they become known. Figure 7-4 illustrates this nifty use of the WBS.

Another application of this technique is cost estimating, which I'll discuss later in this chapter.

WBS Work Package & Cost Account Numbers			Responsible	Effort Required	Resources	Estimated Cost	Precedent Task
Project XYZ							
$785,000	10X-Design $70,900	101-Mechanical	M. Jones	8 Weeks	2 Designers	$20,500	—
		102-Electrical	R. Smith	6 Weeks	2 Technicians	$18,000	101
		103-Software	H. Baker	10 Weeks	3 Programmers	$32,400	101, 102

Figure 7-4. Using the WBS to capture activity data

Identifying Who Does What: The Responsibility Assignment Matrix

The Responsibility Assignment Matrix (RAM) is a tool that identifies how project participants interact with the activities of the project. The most common type of interaction is responsibility for completing an activity. But consider other situations, such as these: a technical expert who must be consulted on several activities, management approvals that are required before initiating an activity, or a client representative who must be notified when certain activities have been completed. The RAM provides an opportunity for documenting these types of people-project interactions. Figure 7-5 illustrates an example of a Responsibility Assignment Matrix.

Along the left of the RAM are the project activities—again, a direct output of the WBS. (These should be elements of work, *not* functional responsibility.) Across the top are the major project participants. (These should be specific individuals. You may indicate just the departments, before individuals are assigned.) In each cell is a letter that denotes the type of people-project

WBS Element	Project Team Members					Other Stakeholders		
	I.B.You	M. Jones	R. Smith	H. Baker	F. Drake	Sponsor	Clnt Mgt	Func Mgt
1.0.1.1 **Activity A**	N				R			
1.0.1.2 **Activity B**		R	C					
1.0.1.3 **Activity C**	R		S			A		G
1.0.2 **Activity D**			R		S			A
1.0.3.1 **Activity E**			R			N		
1.0.3.2 **Activity F**				R				
1.0.3.3 **Activity G**	R				S	A	A	
1.0.4 **Activity H**		R			C	N		

Key: R = Responsible, S = Support Required, C = Must Be Consulted, N = Must Be Notified, A = Approval Required, G = Gate Reviewer

Figure 7-5. Responsibility assignment matrix

interaction. There are no standards for the codes; use whatever works for your particular situation and include a key. Here are some possible interactions:

- Responsible
- Accountable
- Must be notified
- May be notified
- Participant

- Document reviewer
- Input requested
- Approval required
- Support
- Gate reviewer

The RAM can be a valuable communication device, as it displays the project participants and their implied relationship to one another as well as to the project.

Identifying How Long It Will Take to Do Everything (Time Management)

Once you've identified the elements of work (activities), the next major step consists of estimating how long everything will take. First, you estimate how long each activity will take. Then, you combine all of the activities—using logic—in a way that yields an estimate of when each activity is scheduled for completion and how long the entire project should take.

The principal output of this portion of the planning process is a control schedule—an activity-based timeline that the team will use as a map for executing the work and that you'll use as a guide for verifying that work is getting done on time.

Some Basic Definitions

Time management and scheduling involve certain terms that you need to understand. Here are some basic definitions:

Critical Activity An activity that has no latitude in start time and finish time. In other words, if a critical activity does not finish by the prescribed time, the overall project timeline will be impacted.

Critical Path The longest path through the network (logic) diagram. All activities on the critical path are critical activities.

Duration The window of time within which an activity is expected to be completed.

Effort The number of labor hours to be spent on an activity.

Float (or Slack) Flexibility, or latitude, with regard to when a specific activity can (or must) be worked on.

Forward Pass/Backward Pass Techniques for analyzing the amount of float in the execution of individual activities. Activities with no float are referred to as critical activities.

Milestone A point in time, typically marking an important event, usually the completion of a project phase, a decision point, or the completion of a major project deliverable. Milestones are not activities: they don't take time or consume resources.

Network (or Logic) Diagram The model of the proper sequence of activities. It graphically depicts which activities must be completed before others can begin.

Parallel Activities Activities that can be done during the same period of time.

Predecessor Activity An activity that must be completed before the activity under consideration can begin.

Series Relationship Two activities that must be done in a particular order, that is, one must be done before the other.

Preparing a Project Timeline: A Seven-Step Process

There are countless ways to prepare a project schedule. I believe in taking a very systematic approach, which is outlined in this seven-step process. (Details on some of the key techniques will follow.)

Step 1. Prepare for Scheduling by Identifying Schedule Activities on the WBS. Using the WBS, identify the specific activities that will appear on your schedule. You should have already broken down these activities to a level where you can track and control their progress. (Remember the 4% rule of thumb?) You should define each activity in sufficient detail so that all relevant project participants understand the activity completely.

Step 2. Develop the Network Diagram. Prepare a logic diagram that includes all project activities. (We'll discuss this in detail shortly.) Arrange the activities to show any interdependencies by asking two questions:

- Which tasks must be completed before others may begin?
- Which tasks can be done at the same time?

Step 3. Estimate Preliminary Activity Durations. Identify how long each activity would take, assuming full-time commitment and unlimited resources. *Don't panic!* This is done primarily to establish a benchmark of the best possible schedule. You'll make accommodations for limited resource availability in Step 5. Try to obtain estimates of effort from people who are expected to do the work, if possible.

Step 4. Calculate Specific Calendar Dates and Times. You can now use the logic you've developed (the network diagram), your estimated activity durations, and an assumed start date to position the project timeline onto a calendar. Accommodate holidays and other special situations as needed. Calculate a project completion date. Your first iteration will represent the earliest possible completion date.

Step 5. Identify Resources, Accommodate Resource Limitations, and Estimate Final Durations. Secure resource commitments and begin assessing their availability, based upon the current version of the schedule you developed in Step 4. Rework schedule (recalculating dates and times) as needed to accommodate resource constraints, such as part-time participation levels or specific periods of unavailability. You may need several iterations to match resource availability to dates. Additional iterations may be needed as you accommodate external constraints (Step 6).

Step 6. Identify and Accommodate Any External Constraints. External constraints are immovable calendar dates or time periods that must be accommodated. These constraints are imposed from sources outside the project or the project team and are typically beyond your control. Examples may include work done by others (unrelated to the project), reliance on owner-furnished equipment, or limited site availability.

Step 7. Compare the Estimated End Date and the Required End Date. Once you've accommodated all constraints, create a baseline control schedule. Document all assumptions and commitments. If your estimated completion date lies beyond management's expectations, a risk-based approach (commonly called "crashing") may need to be performed. This will be covered in the next chapter.

Creating a Network Diagram

As described above, the first step in the scheduling process actually begins at the end of scope management. It consists of identifying the specific activities that you'll be scheduling. Once you've done this, you're ready to create the network diagram.

The network diagramming process begins by defining the relationships that exist among activities. Some people try to skip this step and attempt to execute their project directly from an activity list. This is the "To do list approach." Although this may work for extremely small projects (20-30 activities with one or two people), it will not work on projects that involve dozens of tasks with multiple players. In most projects, several people are working on different activities at the same time and many activities are dependent upon one another, so it's virtually impossible to manage a project from a list. A network diagram is required.

The most common graphical convention for drawing network diagrams is the Precedence Diagramming Method (PDM). PDM diagrams consist of boxes that represent activities. The relationship between activities is indicated with arrows.

Figure 7-6 indicates that Activity A must be completed before Activity B can begin. This is an example of a *series relationship,* also known as "Finish-to-Start" relationships, for obvious reasons. Series relationships are by far the most common type of relationship.

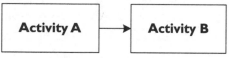

Figure 7-6. PDM series relationship

The other type of relationship occurs when two activities can be done at the same time—a *parallel relationship.* Figure 7-7 illustrates one way of showing a *parallel relationship* in a network diagram. In this example, Activity C and Activity D must both be completed before Activity E can begin.

Note that no relationship is implied between Activity C and Activity D, as there's no arrow connecting them. In some cases, however, a relationship *may* exist between two activities that are to be done in parallel. This type of relationship will link either

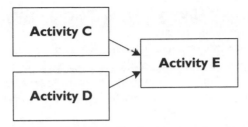

Figure 7-7. PDM parallel relationship

the start or the finish of two activities. Figure 7-8 illustrates these kinds of relationships: a Start-to-Start relationship (a) and a Finish-to-Finish relationship (b).

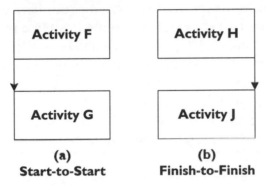

Figure 7-8. PDM parallel relationships

Believe it or not, this is all you need to know to begin constructing your own network diagram.

You'll start by examining your WBS, where you've identified the activities to schedule, track, and control. The process is quite simple. As you consider each individual activity, you begin considering the interrelationships that exist between that activity and others. For each activity, ask the following questions:

- What activities must be completed before this activity can start?
- What activities cannot start until this one is complete?
- What activities could be worked on at the same time as this one?

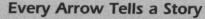

Every Arrow Tells a Story

Smart Managing Pay attention to the direction of the arrows in network diagrams. Although it may seem like a minor point with parallel relationships, there are times it makes a difference. Take a look at Figure 7-8(a) again. The two activities are taking place at the same time, but the direction of the arrow indicates that Activity G can start anytime *after* Activity F starts.

There are several methods for capturing the information on activity interrelationships. You can construct an ordered list, a chart (using the WBS) that you can use to input into scheduling software, or a wall chart.

How about an example? Let's say that our family is preparing for a trip to the ski slopes. We might identify a number of activities—and their relationships—as shown in Figure 7-9. Once again, note that at this point we're not concerned with who's doing the work or how long it will take. Our only objective is to display the logical interrelationships of the project activities.

Using these relationships and PDM graphical conventions described above would yield the simple network diagram shown in Figure 7-10.

Activity Number	Activity Name	Depends on Activity
1	Prepare picnic basket	4,5,9
2	Awake, shower, dress	—
3	Load the car	1,7
4	Make sandwiches	2
5	Make hot chocolate	2
6	Drive to ski slope	8
7	Gather all skiing gear	2
8	Get gas	3
9	Gather munchies	2

Figure 7-9. Activities and interrelationships for the ski trip project

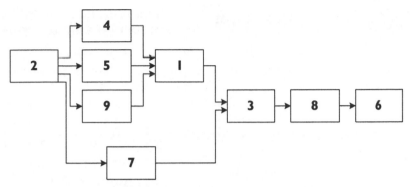

Figure 7-10. Network diagram for the ski trip project

Estimating Activity Durations

Once you've properly modeled the logic with a network diagram, you're ready to move to the next step in scheduling—estimating how long it will take to get the work done. You'll need to use two methods to do this.

The first way to characterize the length of an activity is *effort.* Effort is defined as the *number of labor hours* that task performers will be working on a given activity. You might think of it as the amount of time they'll be charging to your project.

The second way to characterize the length of an activity is *duration.* Think of duration as the window of time within which the activity is to be completed.

Here are some key points about the duration of an activity:

A Sticky Situation!

Here's an excellent (and easy) way to construct a network diagram in "real time." Assemble your entire team in front of a very large wall chart. (Several pieces of easel paper taped on the wall will do just fine.) Put activity titles on sticky notes, one to a sheet. Place activities on the wall in ways that visually display interrelationships: put series activities side by side and stack parallel activities one above the other. When you're satisfied with the general flow of activities (normally left to right across the page), draw in the arrows to indicate all dependencies. Before you know it, you have a network diagram—and a team that fully understands how it was developed. This is a very powerful teambuilding activity.

⚠ CAUTION!

You Need Both

In order to properly manage your project, you will need to understand, quantify, and track both effort and duration. Since effort represents the time people are charging to your project, it relates directly to cost estimating, budget preparation, and cost control. Duration relates directly to schedule estimating, schedule creation, and schedule control.

- Duration is the length of time that you would use for an activity when you place it on your project schedule.
- Duration is derived by considering the effort required to complete an activity, then making appropriate adjust ments for:
  - The quantity of resources assigned to work on the activity (and how efficiently they can work together at the same time)
  - The general availability of the resources (half-time? quarter-time? 10%?)
  - Specific periods of inactivity or unavailability (vacations, site shutdowns)
  - Weekends, holidays
  - Number of hours assumed in each work day

Although duration appears to be a calculated quantity, you should think of it as more of a negotiated figure and a kind of "meeting of the minds" than as a calculation. When you and a given task performer agree on a duration for an activity, it almost represents a contractual relationship—the task performer is promising to finish the task within a window of time and you are accepting that estimate.

Converting the Network Diagram to a Project Control Schedule

In the seven-step process briefly described above, steps 4-6 represent an iterative process that consists of combining the logical relationships you developed through network diagramming, your estimated activity durations, and any known constraints. The final result will be the project control schedule. Think of a control schedule as a logic-based bar chart that has

Ask for Three Pieces of Information

Whenever task performers are providing you with estimates for accomplishing work, you should ask them for at
least these three things:

Smart Managing

1. The amount of effort (or labor hours) required to accomplish the
   task
2. The duration, or window of time within which they will complete
   the activity
3. A basis of estimate—a description of how they determined both
   figures

   You are now in a position to fully understand exactly how these figures were derived. This will help you verify their validity before plugging them into the schedule or budget and help you manage any
changes that may occur as the project progresses.

been "overlaid" onto a calendar and approved by all parties
involved. It provides you with all of the information you will
need to monitor progress and maintain control over the project
timeline. An illustration of the control schedule for our ski trip
project is shown in Figure 7-11.

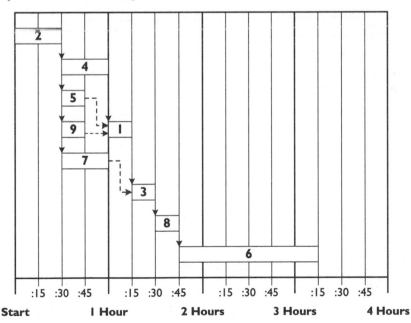

Figure 7-11. Control schedule for the ski trip project

To maximize your understanding of the final product—your project control schedule—I recommend following process steps 4-6 as outlined above. Begin by creating a calendar-based timeline that assumes unlimited resources and the full-time commitment of all task performers. Real-world experience tells us that it's very unlikely that these assumptions will hold true. However, preparing a version of your project schedule using these assumptions *will* provide you with a very useful piece of information—the optimum schedule, that is, the shortest possible overall project duration, assuming no use of overtime or other extraordinary tactics. Having this knowledge at hand could prove helpful if you're working in an organizational environment where constant schedule pressure, arbitrary schedule reductions, or imposed deadlines are the norm.

It will also provide you with a starting point for negotiating resource assignments. You can provide resource providers with a rough idea of when a particular resource may be needed and begin examining resource availability.

Developing your final project schedule development may require several iterations, as there are many factors you'll have to juggle before your schedule comes into balance, becomes feasible, and has the buy-in of all affected parties. Each of these factors will have the effect of extending the baseline schedule you've just developed:

1. The general availability of resources (e.g., half-time, quarter-time, etc.)
2. Specific periods of resource availability (e.g., vacations, other assignments, etc.)
3. Adjustment of durations, due to resource shifts (a different task performer is assigned)
4. Potential "spill-over" into major holiday periods as the schedule is extended
5. External constraints (limited access to the job site, for example)

One other important factor must be addressed as specific

resources are identified
and the project begins to
assume its final form. It
pertains to the fact that the
project logic—which was
derived without regard to
who is executing tasks—
could easily create a situation where a specific task
performer may be expect-
ed to work on several
tasks during the same
period of time. This difficulty must be alleviated
through a technique called *resource leveling*.

> **Resource leveling** A
> scheduling technique that
> addresses the problem of
> over-committed resources by adjust-
> ing the project schedule (typically by
> extending it) when the schedule logic
> places demands on a resources that
> exceed their availability. For example,
> if Activity X and Activity Y were two
> parallel activities that identify Joe as
> the required task performer, resource
> leveling would probably place the two
> activities in series, thus allowing Joe
> to work on both.

Calculating the Critical Path

Once you've prepared your final schedule, you'll naturally begin
thinking about how you're going to maintain control and keep
the project on schedule. Now is the time to start thinking about
the critical path concept. Study the schedule illustrated in Figure
7-11. Do you notice that there's one set of activities that are
continuously tied together with no breaks between them? This is
the critical path.

Although the critical path is fairly obvious in this schedule,
it's much more difficult to spot on larger projects. Normally, an
actual calculation is required to determine the critical path. But
since nearly all scheduling software packages calculate the critical path for you, I won't spend any time working through the
details of how these calculations are made. Briefly, the critical
path is derived by performing two manipulations of the schedule—a forward pass and a backward pass. The forward pass calculates the earliest times (or dates) that activities can start and
finish. The backward pass calculates the latest times (or dates)
that activities can start and finish. Figure 7-12 illustrates how
these calculations may be shown on a simple network diagram.

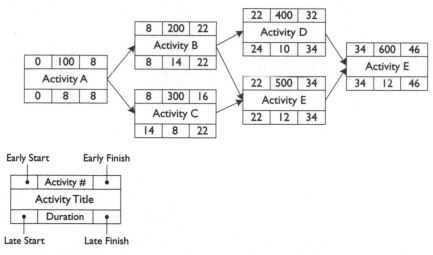

Figure 7-12. Calculation of forward and backward pass

First, a word or two about graphical conventions used in the diagram in Figure 7-12. Again, four dates are calculated for each activity: early start, early finish, late start, and late finish. In this example, these calculations are expressed in terms of the number of days from project startup. On your project, they would most likely be specific calendar dates.

On large projects, you can spot the critical path by examining the difference between the early dates and the late dates. For example, in Figure 7-12, the difference between the early start and late start of Activity C is six days. This means that Activity C could start anytime within this window of time and not impact the overall project schedule. However, notice the difference between the early start and late start of Activity E: zero. This means that Activity E has no flexibility (float) with regard to when it can start. Activity E is on the critical path.

The management implications of being aware of the critical path are obvious. These are the activities that you'll pay the most attention to as you attempt to keep the project on schedule, because one day of slippage in a critical path activity means one day of slippage in the overall project.

One final note about critical path. Remember our discussion

of the importance of keeping your schedule up to date throughout the life of the project? One very good reason for that ties to the critical path concept. It, too, is a "living" entity. In other words, as activities are completed ahead of schedule or behind schedule, the critical path will change. If you don't recog-

Beware of the "Nearly Critical"

Naturally, you must pay close attention to critical path activities. However, watch out for activities that are *almost* on the critical path—those with just a handful of days of float or less. And pay even more attention if these nearly critical activities are difficult, uncertain, or risky. These activities can appear out of nowhere to give you big problems!

nize a change in the critical path through your ongoing schedule updates, you could very likely reach a point where you are spending time, money, and resources fighting fires that don't necessarily matter (i.e., not on the critical path) and *not* addressing your actual problem areas!

Identifying How Much It Costs to Get Things Done (Cost Management)

The third dimension of the project plan is its cost. Cost management, however, is more than just calculating the cost of the overall project. It also consists of creating a budget (identifying the cost of individual elements of work) and the time-scaling of the overall project expenditure, as we'll see. But once again, let's begin with some basic definitions.

Types of Costs

Estimating and budgeting project costs is not as easy as you may think. One reason for that is because there are so many types of costs that you should include in your estimate. Also, there's the overriding issue of direct vs. indirect costs. This is an important distinction that you should understand, so let's clarify.

A *direct cost* is an expenditure specifically and directly incurred by the execution of your project. These are typically the most obvious categories of costs, and include the following:

- **Labor:** The cost of the people carrying out the activities on your project. This could include contract labor. This is often the largest component of the project budget.
- **Materials:** The cost of items purchased for use in executing the project.
- **Supplies and Equipment:** The cost of items consumed by the project and specifically required to execute the project. This item could include items that are purchased, leased, or rented.
- **Facilities:** This would be included only if the facilities are built or purchased solely for the use of the project (in other words, when it's part of what the project delivers).
- **Training:** Training specifically required to achieve project success. This cost is often associated with customer training during installation or startup.
- **Travel and Other Miscellaneous Costs:** Again, the only rule is that the cost must be required to execute the project.

An *indirect cost* is a cost related to supporting the facilities, general services, and organizational environment within which the project team functions. It may include the following:

- **Fringe Benefits:** This is the non-payroll component of workers' salaries for the project. They're often calculated as a simple percentage of direct labor costs and include Social Security costs, health insurance contributions by the organization, and profit-sharing plans, to name a few.
- **Facilities:** The cost incurred to maintain the environment within which the project team functions during the project. This might include building rent, utility costs, building maintenance, communications networks, office supplies, etc.
- **General and Administrative:** The costs of management and support services, such as secretarial, and the purchasing, accounting, and human resources departments, as examples.

In the case of organizations or companies that earn their money through project work, profit would be another necessary component of the project estimate, although not expected to be spent!

Other Nifty Uses for the WBS

Remember our discussion on nifty uses for the WBS? Well, here are two more. The WBS can be used as an estimating worksheet and as your primary structure for displaying the breakdown or allocation of costs within the overall project budget. Let's examine both uses.

Figure 7-13 illustrates how the WBS can be modified to create a fill-in-the-blank worksheet for estimating costs. Its greatest beauty lies in the way it helps you capture the types of project costs, as described above.

WBS Activities with Cost Subtotals	Internal Labor	Material	Contract Labor	Equipment Rent/Lease	Facility Rent/Lease
Project XYZ $785,000 — 10X-Design $70,900 — 101-Mechanical $18,700	$16,500	$1,000	$0	$1,200	$0
102-Electrical $19,900	$17,700	$1,400	$0	$800	$0
103-Software $26,400	$26,000	$2,200	$3,400	$300	$400

Figure 7-13. Using the WBS for cost estimating

Figure 7-14 illustrates how the WBS format serves as an excellent way to show the breakdown of costs. This example takes the WBS to level 3. You'll have to use some discretion in determining whether this is more detail than your management or stakeholders wish to see.

What About Project Management Software?

I've included this topic because it's obviously important. However, I've put it at the end of this chapter for a reason. I believe there's too much emphasis and too much reliance on

Project XYZ $120,000				
	Element 1	$20,000	Activity 1.1	$4,000
			Activity 1.2	$9,000
			Activity 1.3	$7,000
	Element 2	$40,000	Activity 2.1	$12,000
			Activity 2.2	$19,000
			Activity 2.3	$9,000
	Element 3	$25,000	Activity 3.1	$6,000
			Activity 3.2	$11,000
			Activity 3.3	$8,000
	Element 4	$15,000	Activity 4.1	$4,000
			Activity 4.2	$6,000
			Activity 4.3	$5,000
	Contingency	$20,000		$20,000

Figure 7-14. Using the WBS to display project costs

project management software—in particular, scheduling software. Some who are relatively new to project management view scheduling software as the totality of project management. This is very dangerous. Although no one can deny the incredible computing power of scheduling software, an inordinate focus on it belies the breadth of the project management discipline. As we discussed earlier, project planning is so much more than just a schedule. And project management is so much more than manipulating a software tool.

Also, excessive reliance on the tool tends to discount the importance of the "art" part of the project management that we discussed in the beginning of this book. Managing people is the key to project success. However, I recently saw one software

> ### Learn the Basics of Project Management First!
>
> Be sure you understand project management before try-ing to use project management software. If you don't, you could end up in trouble. Remember that using project management software is *not* the same as doing project management; it's just a small extension of it. I once heard a funny but true anecdote: "Using scheduling soft-ware without understanding project management only allows you to create bad schedules—faster."

company advertising that its tool allowed team members to send electronic project status updates to the project manager, thus eliminating the need to get together (as if that were a bad thing). This company was not necessarily targeting the situation of virtual teams—where it's not easy to get together on a regu-lar basis. I think that this is an appalling feature to promote as a benefit for typical project teams.

Selecting the Right Project Management Software

People often ask me the same question: "What's the best project management software?" By now, you should know the standard answer in project management is ... *it depends*. The topic of software selection is no different. It depends upon a number of factors. Here are some of the factors you should consider, exam-ine, and compare before selecting the "right" software for you.

Cost vs. Functionality. The costs and capabilities of project management software vary considerably. Systems can cost anywhere from a few hundred dollars to tens of thousands of dollars. Consider how much power you need with respect to the size of project the software can handle, the features you're likely to need or benefit from. Make sure you keep an eye to the future: consider functionality not only in terms of what you need now, but for the near term as well.

Capability vs. Ease of Use. There's a general relationship between the capability of project management software and its ease of use. I once knew a company whose need for computing power in their project management software was not really that great. However, the decision-makers felt that they wanted maximum horsepower in their software, "just in case." Unfortunately, proper use of the software required sending people off to a month-long, intensive training program and to periodic refresher courses thereafter. The company had difficulty breaking people free to take the training. After two years of hacking their way through the use of the tool, they abandoned it and bought something simpler.

Compatibility with Other Systems. Consider how your project management software will have to interface with other communication, accounting, or reporting systems already in use in your company.

Documentation, Startup Support, and Ongoing Technical Support. How much support can you expect from the manufacturer and/or the company selling the software? Consider important issues, such as the documentation you'll receive, the setup and startup support you can expect, and the long-term technical support you'll get.

Consider using several sources of input, including the experiences of others and rating guides, before making your final selection of project management software.

Words to the Wise About Project Management Software

The tremendous power of project management software can lull you into a false sense of security. Although the tool can save you a significant amount of time, there are many things that it cannot do. You'll have to rely upon your knowledge of project management rather than the tool. Here are some things that the tool cannot do:

- **Make decisions.** You'll still have to determine the course of the project through the day-to-day decisions you make.
- **Gather data.** You must still determine how much data

you need and what forms are most useful to manage
your project.

- **Find errors.** If you input bad data, you will get bad data
out.
- **Solve your most critical problems.** Some of the biggest
problems you encounter will relate to people. Obviously,
project management software does not address this
issue at all.

Project Manager's Checklist for Chapter 7

❑ The first step in the entire detailed planning process is to
identify and break down the work to be done. The work
breakdown structure (WBS) is the preferred tool for doing
this.

❑ Work breakdown structures can be adapted to serve many
planning functions, such as an estimating worksheet.

❑ Preparing a network diagram with your entire team using
"sticky notes" is a very efficient technique—*and* an excellent teambuilding exercise.

❑ There are two ways to characterize the "size" of an activity:
effort refers to how many labor hours will be logged to the
activity (used for *cost* management); *duration* refers to the
window of time within which the activity will be started and
completed (used for *schedule* management). You'll need to
keep track of both!

❑ The critical path is the longest path through the schedule.
There is no margin for error with respect to when these
activities in the critical path can be done. By definition,
delaying a critical path activity means delaying the project.

❑ There are many types of costs. Make sure you've account-
ed for all of them in your cost estimate.

❑ Don't fall into the trap of believing that project management software will manage your project for you. It's simply
a tool.

Dealing with Risk and Uncertainty

B rad pours himself a cup of coffee as he surveys the break room. He's looking for someone he can brag to about the great job he and his team have done putting together a solid project plan. He spots Ted, a veteran project manager, and sits down across the table from him. After a few minutes of discussion about the weather, Ted provides the opening that Brad is looking for.

"So, Brad," says Ted, "How's it going on Project Apex? That's a pretty hot project. I hope you've got everything under control."

"You bet," says Brad as he grins from ear to ear. "The planning took a little longer that I expected, but we've *definitely* got everything under control."

Brad continues by describing some of the details of Project Apex. Ted listens intently as Brad weaves a tale of an intricately crafted schedule, the key project players he's been able to recruit, the "hard bargains" he drove with suppliers, and the well-timed arrangement he worked out with the client for shutting down specific production lines just when he needs them.

"Yes, sir," Brad concludes, "We've got everything nailed down, and we're ready to rip!" Then he adds, "So what do you think, Ted? Not bad for my first time out the chute, eh?"

Brad leans back and awaits affirmation from his experienced colleague.

Ted ponders for a moment, then responds.

"What happens if Alex gets taken off your project? You know how they're always sending him off to the latest trouble spot."

Brad's grin begins to fade.

"And what are you going to do if Accutrex doesn't deliver your parts on time? You've got a backup plan, right?"

"Uhhhh, right," says Brad, the grin now a grimace.

"And what happens if the demand shifts and the client won't let you in to work on the production lines when you want to? You've told management that's a possibility, haven't you?"

"Well, not in so many words," Brad says, excusing himself from the table.

As Brad walks slowly back to his desk, he begins to understand what's happened. In his enthusiasm, optimism, and desire to display a "can do" attitude, he hasn't given enough thought to everything that could go wrong on Project Apex.

Project management is a risky business, Brad thinks to himself as he contemplates his next move. He waits a few minutes—just long enough for Ted to get back to his office—then picks up the phone. Ted has raised some good questions; maybe he can help Brad come up with some answers.

Understanding Risk and Uncertainty

Have you ever seen the toy vehicles that seem to be headed in a particular direction, only to bump into a solid structure and change direction? They continue bumping into things and changing direction until they eventually run out of energy.

If you attempt to lead a project without addressing risk and uncertainty, you'll begin to feel much like one of those toys.

You'll continue to bump into things that will throw you in an unplanned direction. And before long, you'll abandon your original project plan (the one you and your team spent so much time developing) and begin to live by an uncomfortable combination of your wits and the seat of your pants.

Risk and uncertainty are unavoidable in project life and it's dangerous to ignore or deny their impact. Adopting a "can do" attitude may be a good way to get your team members energized and committed, but it's a foolhardy approach when it comes to managing a complex project.

Some Basic Definitions

Let's look at some of the key terms associated with risk management:

Uncertainty Are you surprised that I didn't start with a definition of risk? That's because uncertainty really drives everything else. Uncertainty is defined as *an absence of information, knowledge, or understanding regarding the outcome of an action, decision, or event.* Project managers constantly suffer from an absence of information, knowledge, or understanding.

Risk Risk is actually a measure of the amount of uncertainty that exists. It's directly tied to information, as Figure 8-1 illustrates. This is not exactly the way most of us think about risk in everyday situations. However, in the world of project management, *risk relates primarily to the extent of your ability to predict a particular outcome with certainty.* This interpretation is

Figure 8-1. Risk relationship between information and uncertainty

derived from the study of decision and risk analysis, the statistical sibling to project risk management.

Focus on Threats

With all due respect to the notion of capitalizing on opportunities, your time will probably be better spent focusing on trying to counteract threats. Experience tells us that you'll encounter many more factors that can make things bad for you than factors that can make things better.

Smart Managing

Threat The effects of risk can be positive or negative. Positive effects of risk are often referred to as *opportunities*. *Threats* are the negative—or "downside"— effects of risk. Threats are specific events that drive your project in the direction of outcomes viewed as unfavorable (e.g., schedule delays, cost overruns, and inferior product performance).

Managing Risk: An Overview

Many approaches can be used to address risk and the threats it produces. However, most processes for managing risk tend to follow some variation of this basic four-step approach:

Step 1. Identification (determining what threats exist). Identify all significant uncertainties (sources of risk), including specific threats (also called *potential problems* or *risk events*) that could occur throughout the life of the project.

Step 2. Quantification (determining how big the threats are). Obtain information on the range of possible outcomes for all uncertainties and their distribution and/or probabilities of occurrence, to better understand the nature of the threats and their potential effects on the project.

Risk assessment The combination of risk identification and risk quantification. The primary output of a risk assessment is a list of specific potential problems or threats.

Key Term

Step 3. Analysis (determining which threats are of greatest concern). Use the knowledge gained through risk assessment to determine which potential problems represent the greatest

danger to achieving a successful and predictable project outcome, ordinarily by considering the probability that a specific
problem will occur and its anticipated impact on the project.

Step 4. Response (dealing with the threats). Determine the
best approaches for addressing each high-threat potential problem, which may include evaluating and choosing among a
number of alternatives, and create specific action plans.

Now let's take a closer look at each of these four steps.

Identifying What Can Hurt You

The first step in the risk management process is figuring out
what you're up against. What kinds of things threaten your ability to deliver what you've promised? As mentioned earlier, it all
begins with the uncertainty of not knowing exactly how things
are going to turn out. This is just another way of saying that
many aspects of projects are unpredictable, despite our best
efforts to nail them down. Figure 8-2 lists some of the most
common areas of uncertainty.

From these sources of uncertainty spring problems. Problems are what you need to uncover, specific potential problems,
as many as you can think of. But how do you go about identifying problems? There's no magic formula for identifying potential
threats to your project. It's going to require specific knowledge
of the project, significant brainpower, and the ability to specu-
late. Hmmm....that sounds like an excellent opportunity for a
teambuilding event.

In Chapter 5, we discussed how some of the best teambuilding events are ones where team members expand their knowledge of each other and the project at the same time. Identifying
potential problems as a team is an ideal way to accomplish
that. I characterize the effect of events like this as *building the
collective intelligence of the team.*

Specifically, your approach begins by getting the entire team
together. I recommend reserving at least two to four hours,
depending upon project size and complexity. Gather every piece

Area	Description
Scope	Estimated extent of the work, ability to clearly define work, design errors and omissions, customer-driven scope change
Time	Estimated project duration, estimated activity duration, time-to-market, launch date, timing of management reviews and approvals
Cost	Estimated project costs, downstream manufacturing costs, downstream maintenance costs, inflation, currency exchange, budget limitations
Technology	Customer expectations, probability of success, ability to scale-up, product manufacturability, design success
Resources	Quantity, quality, availability, skill match, ability to define roles and responsibilities
Organizational	Client's priorities and knowledge, coordination among departments
Marketability	User expectations, sales volume, pricing, share, demographics, quality, geography, economy
Outside Factors	Competitor actions or reactions, regulations

Figure 8-2 Typical areas of high uncertainty

of documentation you can and urge others to do the same. Typical background documents may include the Requirements Document, the Project Definition Document, and the business case. (Refer back to Chapter 4 if you're fuzzy on these terms). Of more immediate value will be your project planning documents, such as the WBS, the project control schedule, and the Responsibility Assignment Matrix. Finally, assemble any relevant supporting documentation, such as basis of estimate sheets, planning assumptions, and the network diagram used for schedule development.

The point of all of this is that you want as many documents as possible on hand to help stimulate thinking about potential problems. A checklist can also be quite helpful for stimulating

Project Scope	Facilities and Equipment	Personal
__ Client adds scope or features	__ Lack of availability	__ Vacations/illnesses
__ Work cannot be accurately defined	__ Poor reliability	__ Family/other issues
__ Scope is underestimated	__ Incompatibility w/ existing	__ Conflicting interests
__ Project objectives change	__ Competing uses or users	__ Outside distractions
Project Schedule	__ Proprietary limitations	__ Ethics issues
__ Project duration underestimated	__ Poor flexibility/adaptability	__ Moral issues
__ End date shifts during project	__ Undesirable location	**People/Interpersonal**
__ End date is unrealistic	__ Space (lack of, wrong type)	__ Performance/productivity
__ Project approvals are late	**Resources**	__ Interpersonal conflict
__ Management reviews delay project	__ Team members change	__ Development and growth
Marketing	__ Funding, shifts or freezes	__ Poor motivation and attitudes
__ Unrealistic user expectations	__ Uncertain costs/expenses	__ Poor skills fit
__ Market requirements shift	__ Unavailability of	__ Health and safety issues
__ Price point changes	__ Misaligned priorities	__ Diversity issues
__ Sales volume goes down	**Organizational**	**External Influences**
__ Sales volume goes up	__ Unclear roles/responsibilities	__ Weather, natural disasters
Material	__ Poor delegation	__ Government regulations
__ Source(s) and availability	__ Poor relationships among units	__ Health/Safety/OSHA
__ Poor integration w/ existing	__ Lack of proper coordination	__ Patent, copyright issues
__ Poor supplier reliability	__ Potential turf wars	__ Cultural barriers
__ Poor material reliability	__ Policy limitations	__ Political tensions
__ Substandard quality	__ Poor communications	__ Economic trend shifts
__ High price	__ Line vs. staff issues	__ Poor company image
	__ Reorganization issues	__ Unfavorable legal position

Figure 8-3. Common problems encountered on projects

thoughtful speculation. Figure 8-3 lists over 60 common problems encountered on projects. Consider using this or a similar checklist when meeting with your team.

List as many potential problems as you can, using brainstorming techniques. Although you don't want to stifle creativity, try to keep the list to a reasonable size (perhaps 30-50, depending on project size and complexity).

> **TRICKS OF THE TRADE**
> **Consider Combinations**
> When you and your team are trying to identify potential problems, try not to think in just one "dimension"— that is, one potential problem occurring in isolation. Encourage everyone to think of likely (and lethal) *combinations of problems*. Two specific problems may not represent much of a threat when considered independently, but together may spell disaster.

As you list potential problems that threaten your project, don't lose sight of the concept of uncertainty. Remember that the lack of information, knowledge, and understanding is really your enemy. In other words, think of your biggest "threats" as those that have the greatest potential to throw you off course the furthest—in an unfavorable direction.

Quantifying How Badly You Can Get Hurt

OK, so you've listed a number of things that could go wrong. But how "big" is the threat that they pose? You need to quantify the magnitude of what you're up against. You'll need to spend some time gathering insight on the potential problems you've identified in Step1. This will take some time and judgment, which is why you limit the list of potential problems. There are two basic characteristics you'll want to quantify:

Nature or Extent of the Problem. Let's say that a labor strike is possible. Who would be involved? Just a single work group? The entire plant? When would it happen? Next month? Six months from now?

Nature or Extent of the Effect. Let's say that the same strike could cause "a schedule delay." How much of a delay? A week? Two weeks? A month? Will the project necessarily be delayed by that same amount?

When gathering insight on the nature and extent of problems and their effects, you'll have to rely on several sources, including the following:

- Survey data (preference, opinion, etc.)
- Historical data
- Product specification sheets
- Mockup, simulation, or testing
- Subject matter expert (SME) judgment

Analyzing the Biggest Threats to Your Project

At this point, you and your team have identified a substantial list of potential problems. You've tried to quantify the extent of these problems and their potential effects on your project. Obviously, you don't have the resources to deal with every one of these potential problems. So how do you narrow the list to a manageable size? How do you identify the problems that threaten you the most and therefore demand your attention?

There are a number of methods for shortening the list. One of the most common and straightforward consists of making subjective judgments about two characteristics of potential problems—*probability* and *impact.* These terms mean exactly what you would expect. Probability is the likelihood that the potential problem will occur. Impact is the seriousness or severity of the potential problem in terms of *the effect on your project.*

Once the probability and seriousness have been identified, determining the "high-threat" problems becomes an issue of basic arithmetic. They're the ones that yield the largest number when you multiply probability and impact. (For simplicity, let's call it the "threat rating.") Figure 8-4 offers a graphical representation of this concept.

Responding to high-threat problems will consume resources, so you

> ⚠️ CAUTION!
>
> **Clarify the Terms!**
> When assessing the probability and impact of potential problems, a 5- or 10-point rating scale is often used. Whatever scale you choose, take time to clarify the terms you use. This way, when a team member suggests that the impact is a 3, for example, others will have a sense of what that means. Without this type of clarification, differences in understanding could undermine an already subjective process.

must be prudent in determining how many you choose to take further action on. I recommend using a combination of an agreed-upon number of problems and a predetermined lower limit of threat rating. Below that threshold, you simply won't address problems. (On a 10-point rating scale, somewhere around 30-40 is a reasonable lower limit.) Above the lower limit, you can force rank problems and agree upon how many the team will take further action on. (The top five is probably a reasonable number.)

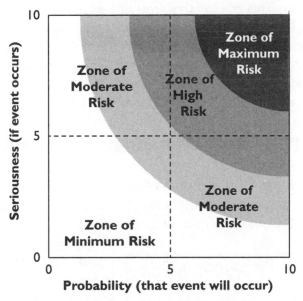

Figure 8-4. Graphical representation of threat ratings

Responding to High-Threat Problems

There are a number of ways to address the high-threat problems you identify. Let's examine *all* of the options for dealing with risk and potential problems:

Avoidance. In avoidance, you choose a course of action that eliminates your exposure to the threat. This often means that you're now pursuing a completely different course from what you'd originally planned. The space shuttle program provides an excellent study in avoidance. Many flights are carefully planned and then, because of marginal weather conditions, scrubbed. Delaying the takeoff of a space shuttle mission because of a weather threat is a perfect example of risk avoidance.

Transfer. The most widely quoted example of risk transfer is something we're all very familiar with—insurance. Risk transfer does not "treat" the risk; it simply makes another party responsible for the consequences of the risk.

Assumption. This means that you are aware of the risk, but choose to take no action on it. You're agreeing to accept its consequences or to simply deal with them if it happens. That's essentially how you're treating threats that fall below the threat rating described above. Assumption is also a valid strategy in situations where the consequences of the risk are less costly and/or less traumatic than the effort required to prevent it.

Prevention. Prevention refers to action taken to *reduce the probability of occurrence* of a potential problem. Ordinarily, it will be your first course of action in dealing with high-threat problems. Prevention begins with identifying the root causes of potential problems. Determining root cause may allow you to identify preventive measures that could reduce the probability that a given problem will occur. Be sure to revise the project plan to incorporate any preventive actions that you intend to take, so that they're not overlooked or forgotten.

> **TRICKS OF THE TRADE**
>
> ### An Ounce of Prevention ...
>
> Prevention is often the least costly and most reliable strategy for dealing with risk—particularly in situations where the impact is high. You should plan and execute preventive measures whenever it makes sense.

Mitigation of Impact. This strategy aims at reducing the negative effects of a problem. You're taking measures to *lessen the impact.* For example, installing air bags in automobiles does nothing to reduce the probability of accidents, but it may significantly reduce the effects. It's important to note that mitigation tactics may be viewed as a waste of time, money, and effort, if the potential problem does not occur.

Contingency Planning. Contingency plans are specific actions that are to be taken when a potential problem occurs. Although they're intended to deal with problems only after they've occurred, *contingency plans should be developed in advance.* This helps ensure a coordinated, effective, and timely response. Also, some plans may require backup resources that need to be arranged for in advance. Contingency planning should be done only for the high-threat problems that remain after you've taken preventive measures.

Managing Project Risk Is a Mindset

Although the process described above is applied

> **Build Warning Mechanisms**
>
> **Smart Managing**
>
> When developing contingency plans, be sure you identify a specific point—"or trigger"—that will alert the project team that it's time to put the contingency plan into effect. It's advisable to incorporate the trigger into the project plan.

specifically to the review and analysis of your project plan, risk and uncertainty require your ongoing attention. Risk management is not just a process—it's a mindset. From the very beginning of your project, risk and uncertainty will be an ever-present threat to your project.

Even though you may feel that you've effectively dealt with risk by using a process such as the one outlined above, some amount of maintenance will be required. The size and shape of threats is continually changing, so you must monitor them on an ongoing basis. Be attentive to any preventive measures to make sure they're addressing the threats as intended. You must remain vigilant for triggers—the points that alert you to the need to pursue a contingency plan. In addition, be on the alert for new threats.

Unfortunately, however, new threats will not necessarily be obvious. You should always be "looking for trouble." Be skeptical, aggressive, and relentless in your quest to uncover potential problems. As the saying goes, if you don't manage risk, it will manage you!

Accommodating Uncertainty

Potential problems—or threats—are specific manifestations of the uncertainty that exists in all projects. Properly dealing with specific threats reduces the downside variability of the final project outcome. In common terms, it is intended to protect your project from harmful events.

However, despite your best efforts to identify and address threats, a large number of circumstances (think of them as little threats) will remain that you won't be able to identify or have the resources to address. Further, too many things can happen that you simply cannot foresee or predict. That's why variability is inherent in projects.

This inherent variability is impossible to manage away. Therefore, you must acknowledge it and accommodate it. Recognize, evaluate, estimate, and communicate its existence to your management and other stakeholders, as appropriate. This module offers some insight on methods for accommodating uncertainty and the inherent variability that goes with it. With luck (and statistics) on your side, the positive and negative variability will even out and you'll end up somewhere near your estimated project targets.

Using "PERT" Calculations to Determine Schedule Durations

The calculations used in the Program Evaluation and Review Technique (PERT) approach recognize the variability inherent in each activity and applies rudimentary statistics in a way that accommodates the variability. PERT calls for three estimates to be provided for each activity:

- **Pessimistic:** the duration if things go poorly
- **Optimistic:** the duration if things go very smoothly
- **Most Likely:** our "best guess"

Figure 8-5 offers more insight on this technique for accommodating uncertainty.

Key Term PERT An acronym for Program Evaluation and Review Technique. Many people erroneously refer to the network diagrams with lines and bubbles as "PERT charts," believing that the bubbles are what make that particular network diagram a PERT chart. What distinguishes the PERT approach from other network diagramming techniques is the use of a *probabilistic approach*. PERT uses statistics to determine activity durations and to calculate the probabilities of specific project outcomes.

The formula often used in conjunction with the PERT diagramming method (although it could be used at any time) is as follows:

$$\frac{O+4M+P}{6}$$ where
O = the **optimistic** estimate of task duration
M = the **most likely** estimate of task duration
P = the **pessimistic** estimate of task duration

Statistically, this formula "favors" the most likely, but allows for some adjustment to accommodate extremes in minimum or maximum outcome.

Sample Calculations:

Optimistic	Most Likely	Pessimistic	Risk-Adjusted Duration
5	7	15	8
8	17	20	16
16	17	30	19

Figure 8-5. PERT technique for accommodating uncertainty

Using Ranged Values When Expressing Estimated Outcomes

The most explicit way of accommodating uncertainty is as much of an issue of style as of mathematics. Whenever you're asked to provide an estimate for *anything,* project management best practice dictates that you should express the estimate as a range of possible outcomes, rather than one specific number.

Try it. The next time you prepare a cost estimate, for example, tell your management this: "I can state to a 95% degree of certainty that the project will cost between $100,000 and $125,000."

Then step back and wait for the reaction. It probably won't be favorable. Unfortunately, it should be, because you've provided some very valuable information. And you've done the best you could, given the uncertainty you're facing. The problem is that people are usually looking for a specific figure. Unfortunately, you cannot—in good conscience—provide a specific figure. Do you remember that uncertainty is defined as an absence of information, knowledge, or understanding regarding the outcome of an action, decision, or event? Well, you're likely to have truckloads of uncertainty at the outset of a project. You should publicize this uncertainty, not mask it behind a single figure—namely, that "best guess" you were asked to provide.

Using Commercially Available Estimating Software

Through the use of the sophisticated estimating software currently available, some of the attitudes and reactions depicted above may begin to change. Several products are on the market now that use the power of statistics to create probabilistic estimates. The capability of these software tools is astounding and well worth mention. They are quite powerful, yet easy to use. Though they vary somewhat in style, most work the same way, following the approach described below. (This is an example for estimating costs; the procedure for estimating a schedule is more complex, but similar in approach.)

Step 1. Estimate Minimum, Maximum, and Most Likely Values. That sounds a little like PERT, doesn't it? Actually, the principle is similar, but, as you'll see, the software tool takes the evaluation to a much greater depth. Figure 8-6 shows a portion of a typical input form.

Step 2. Select the Appropriate Risk Profile. The risk profile is intended to model the most likely distribution of potential costs for each activity. Profile A, for example, is suggesting that the cost of the activity could very well fall anywhere within the overall range. (See Figure 8-7.) A triangular distribution that peaks at the most likely cost is the most common choice, as it represents a very reasonable assumption. Entering data for this step consists of a simple push of a button.

Step 3. Incorporate Any Known Dependencies. In this step, you define any dependent relationships that may exist between activities. This is not a big deal in estimating costs, but would be for scheduling.

Step 4. Run the Simulation. At this point, the statistical software takes your input and simulates the execution of your project as many times as you wish—500 to 1000 is a popular choice.

Task Name	Minimum Cost	Most Likely	Maximum Cost	Risk Profile
1.3 Purchase Materials				
1.3.1 Equipment	$190,000	$200,000	$280,000	A
1.3.2 Electrical	$18,000	$20,000	$24,000	A
1.3.3 Process Control	$27,000	$30,000	$39,000	A
1.4 Installation				
1.4.1 Site Prep	$9,500	$10,000	$20,000	C
1.4.2 Concrete	$22,500	$25,000	$37,500	B
1.4.3 Steel	$27,000	$30,000	$39,000	B
1.4.4 Buildings	$22,500	$25,000	$31,300	D
1.4.5 Equipment	$81,000	$90,000	$126,000	D
1.4.6 Piping	$99,000	$110,000	$137,500	A
1.4.7 Electrical	$81,000	$90,000	$117,000	A
1.4.8 Process Control	$90,000	$100,000	$130,000	B
1.4.9 Coatings	$9,000	$10,000	$12,000	C
1.4.10 Other	$9,000	$10,000	$15,000	C
Total		$1,100,000		

Figure 8-6. Typical PERT input form

Step 5. Evaluate and Interpret the Results. Figure 8-8 illustrates the various outputs that are available.

Figure 8-8(a) is called a *frequency distribution chart*; it
shows how many times your project came in at a given overall
final cost. Note the characteristic shape of a normal distribution.

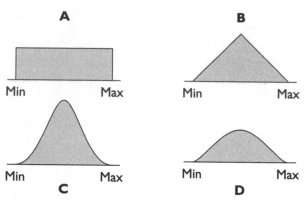

Figure 8-7. Risk profiles

This is fairly common.

Figure 8-8(b) is a *probability curve.* I believe this chart offers the greatest opportunity to illustrate important points when making proposals or presentations. For example, this chart clearly illustrates that there's a 50% chance that the project will exceed $1,118 K. This is not only a statistically sound judgment; it makes a strong point about the concept of ranges and probabilities, when it comes to predicting outcomes. Among other things, it underscores the futility in the use of point estimates.

Finally, Figure 8-8(c) is called a *tornado diagram,* based upon its obvious resemblance to one. This chart illustrates where the uncertainty (and therefore the greatest potential for variability) is greatest.

Together, these graphical outputs—and what they represent—make a strong case for the uncertainty and inherent variability that exists in all projects.

Project Manager's Checklist for Chapter 8

❏ Don't let a "can do" attitude inhibit your ability to understand that bad things can happen to your project. If you don't manage risk, it will manage you

❏ In the world of project management, risk is directly related to uncertainty and the extent to which you can predict a specific outcome or understand the nature of a given situation.

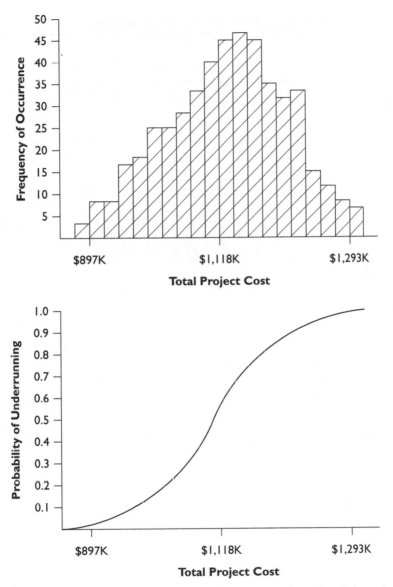

Figure 8-8. Top (a) Frequency distribution chart; bottom (b) proba-bility curve

❑ The focus of your risk management efforts should be on addressing the "downside" effects of risk—or threats.

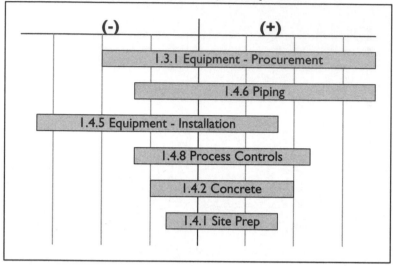

Figure 8-8. (c) tornado diagram

❏ There are four basic steps in managing downside risk:
- identify what threats may exist,
- quantify those threats,
- determine which threats require further action, and
- take action either to reduce the probability that the threat will occur or to lessen its effects if it does.

❏ Perform risk management analyses with your entire team. It represents an excellent teambuilding opportunity.

❏ Not all risk can be eliminated. Sometimes, you must simply acknowledge or accommodate its existence. A good example of this is providing estimates that use ranges of values rather than specific numbers.

❏ Strongly consider the use of commercially available software for cost and schedule estimating. It's a powerful, easy-to-use tool.

Maintaining Control During Project Execution

Brad is ready for project execution. He and his team have prepared a plan and examined potential risks. Now it's time to get down to work. Brad's biggest concern at this point is to keep Project Apex headed in the right direction. As he considers the complexity of his project, questions begin to swirl around in his mind ....

"Am I supposed to be telling everybody what to do all the time?"

"Should I just wait for problems to pop up?"

"How often should I get the team together?"

"What exactly am I supposed to be *controlling*?"

Once again, Brad begins to feel overwhelmed.

"I had no idea that project management was this challenging," Brad mutters to himself.

Then he remembers his colleague, Ted, who helped Brad understand risk management. Once again Brad picks up the phone and dials Ted's number.

What Project Control Really Means

The term *control* has several meanings. Those new to project management are initially dismayed by the use of the term "control," because they mistakenly equate it with the concept of authority. In the world of project management, control has very little to do with telling people what to do, dictating their actions or thoughts, or trying to force them to behave in certain way—all of which are common interpretations of control.

In project management, the term "control" is much more analogous to steering a ship. It's about continually making course adjustments with one main objective in mind—bringing the ship into safe harbor, as promised at the start of the voyage. And the successful project voyage includes identifying a specific destination, carefully charting a course to get there, evaluating your location throughout the voyage, and keeping a watchful eye on what lies ahead.

The Objective of Project Control

Fledgling project managers (and some experienced ones!) often make the same mistake when trying to keep control of their projects. They get wrapped up in the here and now—the measurement and evaluation of their immediate situation—to the exclusion of everything else. They calculate their current position and how far off course they are. That's what they report to management and promise to fix. Their entire focus consists of staying on the line they've drawn from the beginning to end of the project. Unfortunately, controlling the destiny of your project is not that simple.

As we'll see, evaluating where you are in terms of where you're supposed to be is certainly part of the overall control and "getting back on track" is almost always a sound strategy. But your primary mission is to deliver what you've promised, so you should think of "maintaining control" in terms of *minimizing the distance between where you end up and where you said you'd end up.*

This means that overall project control requires an eye on the future, as this formula shows:

Calculated Present Variance + Estimated Future Variance
= Final Project Variance

Maintaining proper control really requires that you consider three parameters: (a) where you are, compared with where you're supposed to be; (b) what lies ahead that can affect you; and (c) where you're going to end up, compared with where you said you would end up. Bear in mind that (a) and (b) are used primarily as *internal control functions* (although you may choose to report them outside the team). They're used for evaluating (c). At the risk of being repetitive, your primary focus should always be on *evaluating where you think you're going to end up.*

There are two reasons for this.

First, you must take intelligent and meaningful corrective action with the end point in mind. Guiding the ship must include more than just steering it back on course; it must also include recognizing that there's an object up ahead that you're going to have to steer around or winds around the upcoming point of land that have kicked up since you started your voyage. The future will always be different than expected at the outset of the project. Assumptions will be revised, operating conditions will change, and new things will be thrown in your path. Sometimes, actions you take now must compensate for future sources of variance as well as variances created though past performance.

The second reason you need to focus on the end point pertains to management reporting. In most cases, what will probably interest them most is a prediction of where you think you're going to end up: this is the type of information they need to run the business. Being able to report to your management that you're two weeks behind schedule or $10,000 over budget *right now* may or may not be of value to them. Reporting that you expect the project to be *completed* three weeks late or $15,000 over budget is much more likely to be of value.

What Are You Actually Controlling?

At this point, you're probably saying, "OK, so I should be focused on the end point of the project and I should be trying to 'get back on track' and minimize variances. But the end point of *what*? Get back on *what* track? And *what* kind of variance are we talking about?" All good questions.

The answers to these questions will take us back to the discussion in Chapter 2 about *the dimensions of project success*. The most fundamental measure of project success relates to meeting the agreed-upon targets in each of these dimensions. These are the targets that you promised to meet at the beginning of the project; these are the targets that you should focus on controlling.

Two of the targets pertain to the consumption of resources:

- Schedule: Was the project completed *on time*? (How long did we take?)
- Cost: Did the project come in *at cost*? (How much did we spend?)

The other two targets are tied to the deliverables of the project:

- Functionality: Do project deliverables have the expected *capability*? (What can they do?)
- Quality: Do the deliverables perform *as well* as promised? (How well can they do it?)

As far as many organizational managers are concerned, the ideal end point occurs when a project meets these four targets exactly as promised. Although "beating targets" is often characterized as desirable, hitting targets provides a level of *predictability* that most organizational managers value. The first two targets (schedule and cost) often get the most attention; hence the very common phrase "controlling cost and schedule."

Sometimes, however, controlling cost and schedule gets too much attention and deliverable performance is not as closely monitored as it should be. This is a major oversight, one that you should concentrate on avoiding. We'll examine methods for

Pay Attention to Deliverable Performance!

Meeting cost and schedule targets can often receive an inordinate amount of a project manager's attention. But if the quality and functionality of the project deliverables is not monitored and maintained, an inferior product may be delivered to an unhappy customer. As part of your project control efforts, continually verify that the standards of deliverable performance that you promised are being maintained. There's truth in the old adage: "They might forget if it cost too much or took too long, but they'll never forget if it doesn't work!"

keeping control over all four of these dimensions of success as we move ahead.

Required Process Elements

Detailed project plans are created to satisfy two basic objectives: first, to provide a map for the project team to follow during project execution; and second, to provide you with an instrument you can use to evaluate whether or not the project is staying on course. Simply stated, you won't be able to maintain control over the project if you do not have a credible and properly detailed plan.

Your ability to evaluate progress on your project, calculate your variance from plan, and predict the future depends upon a number of key process elements. Among these elements are the following:

- A baseline of measurement
- Processes and methods for gathering data
- An ability to get good data
- An emphasis on timeliness
- Processes, tools, and methods for analyzing past, present, and future performance

Let's examine each in more detail.

How Do You Establish a Baseline of Measurement?

The baseline of measurement is actually represented by your project plan. This includes your control schedule, project budget, and any design or performance specifications related to project deliverables. The estimates embodied in these documents create the basis from which variance is measured.

The fact that the baseline is an estimate, however, poses a problem with regard to maintaining control.

What if an estimate is wrong? What if an element of your baseline is a poor representation of what's actually achievable?

When you encounter a variance, it can sometimes be difficult to know whether it's because of the estimator or because of the task performer. *This can be one of the greatest difficulties in maintaining proper control.* Knowing the source of the variance is very important. If you're able to distinguish an *estimating* problem from a *performance* problem, you're in a better position to take the appropriate corrective action. Unless you uncover specific estimating errors, however, you should assume that your baseline is reasonably accurate and use it as your basis for measuring variance and taking corrective action.

What Information Do You Need?

So exactly what kind of information should you be gathering to evaluate your current variance and to maintain control of your project? Below are listed the specific pieces of information you should be requesting.

Schedule:
- Date that each completed activity was scheduled to start and finish
- Date that each completed activity actually started and finished
- Anticipated start date of each activity currently under way
- Actual start date of each activity currently under way
- Originally scheduled completion date of each activity currently under way
- Estimated completion date of each activity currently under way
- Description of the progress made on each activity currently under way

Cost:
- Estimated expenditure (or labor hours) for all activities
- Actual expenditure (or labor hours logged) for each completed activity
- Amount spent to date (or labor hours logged) on each activity currently under way
- Estimated cost to complete (or additional labor hours required) for each activity currently under way

Functionality:
- Estimated (originally envisioned) capabilities of final deliverables
- Current prediction of what capabilities will actually be

Quality:
- Original estimation of how well final deliverables will function
- Current prediction of how well they actually will function

How Do You Gather Information?

Obviously, you have to gather a lot of information and keep track of many things throughout the life of the project. How do you go about getting this kind of information? What processes and methods can you use? Among the most common ones are the following:

Team Meetings. As you can see from the list above, project analysis consists of elements of the past, the present, and the future. The main conduit of current information is ordinarily your project team status meetings. As mentioned earlier, project team meetings should be conducted regularly throughout the life of the project. Figure 9-1 illustrates how choosing a reasonable team meeting frequency yields three groups of activity updates.

Past information consists of recording actual results of completed activities. This is the first order of business. The second order of business—and the main focus of most team meetings—

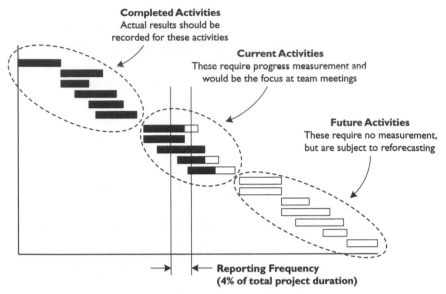

Completed Activities
Actual results should be
recorded for these activities

Current Activities
These require progress measurement and
would be the focus at team meetings

Future Activities
These require no measurement,
but are subject to reforecasting

Reporting Frequency
(4% of total project duration)

Figure 9-1. Choosing meeting frequency

is a thorough review and analysis of the condition of each activity currently under way. Finally, you should always have your eye on the future by asking for information on the predicted outcome of each activity. (We'll discuss this aspect in more detail later in this chapter.)

Forms and Templates. A number of methods exist for gathering information. Among the most straightforward and reliable methods is simply to provide your team members with fill-in-the-blank forms and templates. If the forms and templates are designed properly, they should make life easier for team mem-

CAUTION!

Focus on Reasons and Benefits
Designing and using forms and templates to gather information requires consideration and thought. Whenever you ask people to do something that may seem to them to be additional work (such as regularly filling out data input forms), you must help them understand why you're asking them to do it and how it will make their life easier. If you fail to do this for the forms you create, team members will view them as "busy work" and are likely to resist this process or ignore it.

bers and help to ensure that you get the type of information you need—in the form in which you need it—to maintain control.

Consider designing a WBS-based spreadsheet with spaces for providing input such as labor hours spent, current status, forecasted values, issues or problems, re-estimates of duration and cost, and so forth. You could also provide copies of the project schedule that team members can mark up as appropriate to provide information on current status. There are various possibilities for enabling your team members to give you information; whatever you choose, make sure you take the time and effort to make their lives (and yours) easier.

MBWA. Management by Walking Around (MBWA) may seem cliché, but for effective project leadership it's absolutely vital. Maintaining control is often more than just recording information. It's assessing the motivational level of your team members, evaluating or confirming the accuracy or validity of the information you receive, and uncovering problems or issues that may not surface in a team setting. Sometimes, these things can be evaluated only by spending time with team members, one on one.

Take the time and find ways to spend time with the individuals on your team. Join them in the break room or cafeteria or at lunch from time to time. Call them or seek them out, just to see how things are going. You may be surprised at what you learn.

Software and Systems Support. The information management component of gathering information varies widely from

---

The Value of Informal Communication Methods

Savvy project managers have discovered that information gathered through informal channels of communication can often be more valuable than information gathered through more formal methods, such as team meetings. There are at least two reasons for this. First, some team members may be reluctant to reveal information in front of the entire team that may be of a sensitive nature. Second, a project manager who spends time with individual team members demonstrates concern and is likely to promote a healthier, more open relationship with each team member. You should strive to provide team members with opportunities to communicate with you and transfer information informally.

organization to organization. On some projects, project control documentation may be effectively managed through the use of pencil and paper. Others may make use of sophisticated, company-wide, mainframe systems. The amount of software and systems support you use for your projects will depend on various factors, some of which we examined in Chapter 7, in discussing the amount of planning you should do:

- project complexity
- project size
- organizational expectations
- organizational support (i.e., what the organization provides for you)

Many project managers find themselves somewhere in the middle of the continuum of software and systems support. They use one of the many stand-alone software packages, most of which have a respectable amount of processing capability, but still require manual data entry.

How Do You Make Sure You're Getting Good Information?

To evaluate your position and maintain control, it's not enough to simply gather information. What you need is high-quality information. But what does "high quality" mean? The information you need should be:

In the appropriate form. This means that the information is expressed in a way that allows you to process it with relative ease. How do you ensure that you get information in a form that you can use? First, make your expectations clear regarding the way the information should be presented. Second, as mentioned above, provide forms and templates that team members can simply fill in.

Timely. Your ability to react to problems in a timely manner will depend upon the "freshness" of the information you receive. Since the most of that information will come in team meetings, it follows that the frequency of team meetings is critical. As mentioned earlier, I recommend a team meeting interval of about 4%. In other words, a reasonable frequency for a six-month project would be once per week; for an 18-month project it would be enough to meet once every three weeks, unless there were special circumstances that dictated more frequent meetings. The practice of MBWA described above will also help you receive fresh information.

Precise. I've sat in many team meetings and observed project managers attempting to ascertain the status of current activities. The responses sound like this: "I'm doing OK," "I'm on schedule," "I'm about half done," "I have a little bit more to do and then I'll be done." Needless to say, updates like these do not provide the project manager with enough information to do the job. Refer back to the section in this chapter entitled "What Information Do You Need?" Note that these items request *specific* dates, durations, and dollar amounts. You'll need this type of specific information to maintain proper control.

Credible. The credibility of the information you receive is more closely tied to human nature than administrative processes and methods. There is often a correlation between the validity of the information you receive from team members, and the quality of your relationship with them. The issue often revolves around how comfortable a given team member feels in giving you honest and accurate information—*particularly when things are not going well.*

This comfort level is closely tied to the climate you create and the tone you set—in particular, how you react to "bad news" (unfavorable status reports). Figure 9-2 lists some "Do's and Don'ts" for setting up an open, honest, and credible information flow between you and the members of your team, so you get quality information from your team.

How Do You Analyze the Information?

As mentioned above, your analysis should deal primarily with schedule, cost, functionality, and quality. Let's take a closer look at how to process and interpret the information you receive—

- **DO** reward people for following appropriate processes, even if their results are not always favorable.

- **DON'T** shoot the messenger of unfavorable information, even if the messenger is responsible.

- **DO** encourage and support an "early warning" mentality in reporting.

- **DON'T** spend any time placing blame when poor results are reported.

- **DO** immediately move into a mode of collaborative problem-solving when problems surface.

- **DON'T** ever play one team member against another, or criticize one team member while talking to another.

- **DO** demonstrate personal commitment and accountability.

Figure 9-2. Project management do's and don'ts

and analyze your position—in each of these areas.

Analyzing the Schedule

Schedule analysis relies heavily upon graphic techniques. Figure 9-3 shows a basic project control schedule, where three characteristics are displayed for each activity: the original baseline plan, the amount of progress made, and the forecasted time-to-complete.

The specific configuration of position and shading illustrated in this figure would have been determined by input gathered at a team meeting. Figure 9-4 displays the type of information that

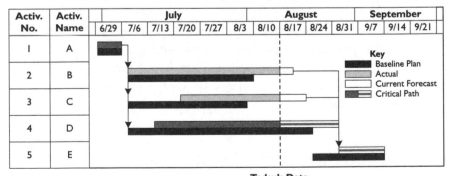

Today's Date
(Date of team meeting)

Figure 9-3. The do's and don'ts of getting high quality data

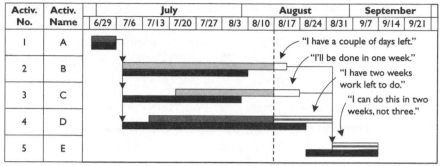

Activ. No.	Activ. Name	July						August				September		
		6/29	7/6	7/13	7/20	7/27	8/3	8/10	8/17	8/24	8/31	9/7	9/14	9/21
1	A													
2	B													
3	C													
4	D													
5	E													

"I have a couple of days left."

"I'll be done in one week."

"I have two weeks work left to do."

"I can do this in two weeks, not three."

Today's Date
(Date of team meeting)

Figure 9-4. Information to develop control schedule

task performers would have provided, to arrive at the control schedule shown in Figure 9-3.

Recording and displaying the information you receive from task performers is little more than "plugging in" status information. This simple and straightforward method will probably be adequate for many projects.

Interpreting control schedules is also straightforward—if they're properly constructed. An analysis of Figure 9-4 allows us to make several observations about the past performance and current status of every activity shown on this control schedule. For example:

> **"Decorating" Your Schedule**
>
> When it comes to choosing schedule graphics, there really aren't any standards for coloring, shading, or patterns; you can choose any scheme that suits you. Most scheduling software applications allow you to select from a large menu of choices for color or shading. Just be sure your choice of colors and patterns is not distracting!

- Activity A started and finished on time.
- Activity B started on time and has taken longer than expected.
- Activity C started two weeks late and the duration hasn't changed.

- Activity D started about a week late and the duration hasn't changed.
- Activity E is scheduled to start as soon as Activity D is completed and will take a week less to complete than originally estimated.

We can also make some *overall* observations regarding our project. Applying the critical path concept discussed in Chapter 7, we're able to see that—although Activities B, C, and D are all running late—only Activity D represents a problem for us, as it's a critical path activity. We can also see, by comparing the baseline and forecast data for Activity E (the last activity in the project), that the combination of all variances equals zero. In other words, we expect to finish on time.

Analyzing Costs

Classic cost analysis used to rely upon charting the actual project expenditure against the anticipated project expenditure. The result would be a graphic similar to the one shown in Figure 9-5.

Although this technique provides a good snapshot of your overall cost position at any time, it has two major drawbacks. First, it does not provide detail at the activity level. This creates a challenge for management, as you cannot determine which

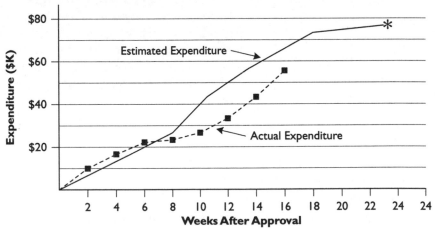

Figure 9-5. Classic cost analysis

activities (if any) are of greatest concern. Second, it does not provide an integrated approach: it's not tied to accomplishment. It tells you how much you've spent (cash flow), but it doesn't tell you what you've gotten for your money (value). This issue will be discussed in more detail in the next section, "The Earned Value Concept."

You can analyze your cost position at the activity level in a manner quite similar to schedule analysis. The process consists of examining the past, present, and future in order to determine your end point (Figure 9-6).

Figure 9-6 illustrates a straightforward method you can use to construct a cost analysis spreadsheet. For each activity, information is tracked for baseline (original estimate), current expenditure, and anticipated future expenditure. Comparing the forecasted total with the original estimate yields a calculated variance for each activity.

Determining the actual expenditure to date for each activity can be quite difficult, however. Inadequate systems support or labor-charging methods may make accurate cost tracking near-

Project Apex Cost Summary
(Actual costs through xx/xx/xx)

Task ID	Baseline Estimate	Spent to Date	Cost to Complete	Revised Forecast	Under (Over)
001	$20,000	$4,250	$16,100	$20,350	$(350)
002	$6,700	$1,150	$5,700	$6,850	$(150)
003	$3,900	$700	$2,900	$3,600	$300
004	$14,600	$10,330	$4,050	$14,380	$220
005	$3,000	$0	$3,000	$3,000	$0
006	$4,200	$2,100	$1,900	$4,000	$200
007	$13,300	$13,500	$1,300	$14,800	$(1,500)
008	$11,500	$2,300	$8,800	$11,100	$400
Total	**$77,200**	**$34,330**	**$43,750**	**$78,080**	**$(880)**

Figure 9-6. Analyzing your cost position

ly impossible. Some project managers track their effort by manually logging labor hours into a cost and schedule management software tool. Though doing this allows them to track costs, it can be an extremely labor-intensive process.

An Integrated Approach to Analyzing Schedule and Costs: The Earned Value Concept

The techniques described above are very helpful in examining your schedule position and your cost position. However, performing a separate analysis of schedule and cost does not provide an entirely accurate or comprehensive picture of overall project status. Evaluating how much work you're getting done without considering how much you've paid to get that work done will give you a distorted picture of your cost position. Similarly, using your rate of expenditure as a measure of project status will lead to a distorted picture of your schedule position.

Take another look at Figure 9-5. It appears as if we're under budget by about 10%. Good news, right?

What if I tell you that the project is nearly completed? Good news becomes unbelievably great news: we're nearly done and we've spent only about three-quarters of the money.

Now imagine that the team has just barely gotten started; not much of anything has been done. This would be a disastrous situation.

In each case, the expenditure is identical. What's different? *The amount of work that's been done.*

The *earned value concept* integrates schedule and cost. There are a number of formulas associated with rigorous earned value techniques. Also, many books deal with the topic of earned value in great detail. For our purposes, however, we'll stay at the conceptual level.

At the core of the earned value technique are these three basic components of measurement:

- Budgeted Cost of Work Scheduled
- Budgeted Cost of Work Performed
- Actual Cost of Work Performed

Budgeted Cost of Work Scheduled (BCWS) is a measure of *what you expect to accomplish.* Specifically, it uses the original cost estimates for activities to chart the cost (or value) of the work that you plan to get done over time. It's equivalent to the conventional concept of the "planned budget." In Figure 9-5, the "Estimated Expenditure" solid line is the Budgeted Cost of Work Scheduled.

Budgeted Cost of Work Performed (BCWP) is a measure of *the value of what you've actually accomplished.* It charts the cost (or value) of the work you've gotten done at any point in time. Again, the original activity-based cost estimates are used to perform these calculations. This is what "earned value" actually is.

Actual Cost of Work Performed (ACWP) refers to *what you paid for what you've accomplished.* This would be your actual cost expenditure at any point in time. In Figure 9-5, ACWP is represented by the "Actual Expenditure" dotted line.

And so, conceptually, your schedule position is a comparison of BCWP and BCWS. In other words (using the terminology above), it compares *what you expected to accomplish* and *what you've actually accomplished,* in terms of originally estimated dollar amounts.

Evaluating your *schedule* position in this manner is somewhat superfluous, as you can do the same thing by using the schedule analysis techniques described earlier in this chapter.

However, using this method to evaluate your *cost* position can be quite informative, as it considers accomplishment. Your cost position can be evaluated by comparing BCWP and ACWP, in other words, *what you thought you'd have to pay* and *what you've actually paid—for a given amount of accomplishment.*

Even if you don't use rigorous earned value techniques, one of the most valuable by-products of earned value is formally evaluating progress through the use of *physical progressing* methods.

You do this by breaking down an activity into smaller parts and then making an assessment of how much progress is being made on an incremental basis. Figure 9-7 illustrates three

Physical progressing A way of expressing accomplishment in tangible, verifiable terms. For example, one of your team members may report being "50% complete" on a major piece of work. How can you tell? If you're using physical progressing methods, the task performer is expected to produce something (a deliverable, if possible) that will substantiate that he or she has reached the agreed-upon level of accomplishment. By doing this, you and the task performer can more accurately judge whether 50% is a fair evaluation of status.

methods for physical progressing.

Determining the best application depends upon the nature of the activity being measured. Using techniques such as physical progressing helps ensure that you and your team members understand progress in the same way. It also sends a message that you'll be *measuring* progress, not just *recording* it.

Type of Measurement	How it Works	Normal Application
Units Completed	If there were five equal tasks, finishing one equates to 20% complete, finishing two equates to 40% complete, and so forth.	Used when a major activity consists of a number of equal or nearly equal tasks, each requiring about the same amount of effort to complete.
Incremental Milestone	25% 50% 75% 100%	Choose arbitrary, incremental checkpoints, then determine the progress that should be made by those points.
Weighted Milestones	Spec'd Designed Built Installed 20% 50% 80% 100%	Used when phases exist within a major activity. It's not necessary for milestones to be equally spaced.

Figure 9-7. Three methods for physical progressing

Analyzing Deliverable Performance (Functionality and Quality)

Analyzing the deliverables of the project—in particular, whether they will meet functionality and quality targets—can be difficult.

In many cases, deliverables cannot be fully evaluated until they've been created. From the standpoint of project control, your mission is primarily to keep deliverable performance from being degraded. It's important to note that deliverable performance can fall short for two reasons.

Failure to Perform as Expected. It's very possible to create deliverables "according to design or specification" that do not turn out as expected. Perhaps they do not perform as we'd hoped or cannot accomplish their intended purpose. This kind of outcome is not uncommon in situations where you're creating something new, where significant research and development is required. In this situation, risk management and communication can be two useful strategies. Make sure that the customer of the deliverables is fully aware that performance problems are a possibility.

To defend against last-minute disappointment or rework, you might conduct periodic checks of deliverables against design specifications, create mockups or sample products, perform random tests, sample representative deliverables, and conduct specially designed performance tests.

Performance Standards Are Altered During the Project. Sometimes a decision is made during the project to lower the standards of performance of project deliverables. This situation can occur if it's determined that what was thought to be achievable is simply not. In other cases, standards are lowered to compensate for cost or schedule problems.

From a management standpoint, the difference between these two situations is huge. An inability to meet performance standards because of technological challenges is often understandable. If handled properly, that is with the understanding and cooperation of the customer, this situation should not become a reflection on your management ability. However, if you or a member of your team "trade off" deliverable performance as a way to save time or money—*without the express permission of the client*—you're asking for trouble. Make sure that you review with your customer any potential modifications to performance standards. And make sure that team members understand that this is never their decision to make alone.

How Should You React to the Information?

OK, you've gathered information and done some analysis. Now it's time to react.

If everything is going well, little reaction is necessary. Most of the time, any action you might be inclined to take would be in response to an undesirable situation. This is commonly known as taking *corrective action*.

> **Key Term**
>
> **Corrective action** Measures taken to get a project back on track. It typically pertains to action taken to remedy an unfavorable set of circumstances (schedule delay, cost overrun, performance issue).

When steering a ship, knowing what to do to get back on course isn't very complicated. Not so with project work. You've got people, processes, and technology to worry about. You're dealing with dimensions that are interdependent (cost, schedule, functionality, and quality). And there may be many strategies for getting your project headed in the right direction.

There is no "right" way to take corrective action. Choosing the best course of action is purely situational: you must carefully consider many factors, including the following.

Know when to take action. This is one of the most difficult aspects of corrective action. There's an old adage: "A project slips one day at a time." Does that mean you should take action as soon as your project falls one day behind? Probably not. But it does suggest that you should not ignore that situation. Early detection is critical to keeping your project from straying too far off course. This is one of the reasons that regular team meetings are so valuable.

Keep a sharp and watchful eye on a situation—and make sure that *task performers know* you're keeping an eye on it.

Brad Learns a Lesson

In one of the project team meetings, Carol reports that software coding is falling behind.

"It's more difficult than I'd originally envisioned," she says as she gives Brad the bad news.

"That activity is supposed to be completed by the end of the month, you know," Brad notes, checking the schedule. "I'll see if I can get you some help, Carol." He then moves on to the next agenda item before Carol can respond to his suggestion.

The very next day, Brad gets a temporary programmer assigned and feels confident that he's resolved the problem.

In the next team meeting, Carol reports that she's fallen even further behind.

That's a surprise for Brad. "What about the programmer I got for you?"

"Sorry, Brad," Carol says. "It took several days just to orient him to Project Apex and what we're trying to do with this program. He only just started being productive a few days ago!"

"Well just finish up as soon as you can," Brad says, having learned a valuable lesson about "throwing bodies at problems."

And sometimes a simple "nudge" in the form of a reminder (e.g., "Don't forget you're supposed to be done in two weeks") is all that's required, if an issue is detected early enough. The worst thing you can do is to ignore a situation, believing that somehow the team will make up the lost time by the end of the project. This simply won't happen unless you make it. Problems rarely work themselves out: you must take action to fix them.

Decide whether to fix the problem (immediate action) or compensate for it (future action). When problems occur, we're often tempted to fix them immediately. However, in many situations, this will not be the right thing to do.

You can sometimes solve problems with immediate and direct action. However, you cannot assume that this should always be your first course of action. Many times, in fact, your best course of action will be to deal with the present as well as you can and look to counteract the effects of the problem through future actions. If you choose to address the problem through future action, be sure to keep everyone informed and to modify the project plan to reflect your actions.

Avoid the micromanagement pitfall. If you're very action-oriented (as many project managers are), you may be tempted to jump into any problem as it occurs. You may justify your action by saying, "I'll get involved only long enough to get the problem under control. Then I'll back off."

You should avoid this temptation, except possibly in serious or extreme situations. First, you simply won't have enough time to jump into every problem that surfaces. Second—and more important—you'll slowly cause your team members to resent your interventions. By getting personally involved, you're sending a message that you do not trust team members to resolve problems on their own.

Your best course of action is to remind them of the need to correct the problem, suggest a remedy (if appropriate), and offer yourself as a resource for support. This demonstrates trust and frees you to spend your time managing issues pertaining to the overall project.

Choose the best recovery strategy. Typically, there are many courses of action you can take to recover from difficulties and try to ensure that the team meets critical project targets. Among your basic options are those listed below, not in any particular order except for the first and last options.

- *Push for compliance.* In most cases, your first course of action should be to try to maintain the original plan. In other words, don't simply assume that potential changes should automatically be accepted or accommodated. Sometimes a firm reminder of the commitment and an offer of support may be enough to stimulate better performance.
- *Recover in later tasks.* As mentioned above, this is often a better option than attempting to fix the immediate problem. Be sure that future plans are reflected in the project schedule.

- *Add resources.* Get additional help. Be sure to consider the potential increase in project expenditure—and the possibility of diminishing returns when resources are added. Having three times the resources on an activity doesn't necessarily mean it will be completed in one-third the time.
- *Accept substitutions.* When something is unavailable or expected to be delivered late, consider substituting a comparable item. Be sure to consider any potential effects on deliverable performance.
- *Use alternative work methods.* Sometimes it's possible to find a more expedient way to accomplish the work. However, changing work methods often has an effect on cost and/or schedule.
- *Accept partial deliverables.* Delivery of only some of the items you need may allow you to keep the project moving forward.
- *Offer incentives.* Offer a bonus or other inducement to improve performance. This strategy is often directed at suppliers. Penalty clauses may have the same effect, but are negative.
- *Renegotiate cost and schedule targets.* Explore the possibility of extending the deadline or increasing the budget, if it helps. This will probably be easier if you can show that problems are due to estimating errors rather than performance issues.
- *Reduce scope.* Reduce the quality and/or performance requirements of the project deliverables so as to reduce the work required. This should ordinarily be your last course of action, when maintaining cost or schedule targets is of paramount importance. It's imperative that all stakeholders agree before you take this course of action.

Understand tradeoffs. As mentioned earlier, the dimensions of schedule, cost, functionality, and quality are interdependent. This means that taking corrective action may involve "trading off" one dimension for another. For example, adding resources may allevi-

Interviewing Techniques

Determining stakeholders' priorities for schedule, cost, functionality, and performance targets can be difficult at times. One method that often yields good results consists of using an interviewing approach. Ask them hypothetical questions, such as "What if the project were to overrun by $20,000?" or "What if we ran into problems and were three weeks late?"

Take note of their answers—and their body language. This will often provide you with insights for making intelligent tradeoffs if you need to take corrective action.

ate your schedule problems, but will probably increase costs. Using less expensive materials may save money, but could affect the functionality or quality of the project deliverables.

It follows, then, that you cannot always protect the integrity of all four dimensions at once. But which dimension(s) should you favor? This is exactly the question you should ask of key stakeholders—particularly the customer—at the outset of the project. Many times, they'll have a preference.

If you're lucky, stakeholders will express their preferences: "I want you to hold the schedule, even if it the costs run over" or "If you need to take more time to make sure this thing works, do it!"

Unfortunately, not all stakeholders are this explicit. However, if you simply spend time discussing the project with them, you'll often come to understand what their preferences are.

Learn from all problems. Simply resolving a problem when it occurs is not enough. One of the habits you should get into is pausing to reflect on the problem you've just encountered. Ask yourself (and others) key questions, such as the following:

- Could this problem happen again?
- If so, can we prevent it? How?
- If we can't prevent it, can we mitigate its effects?
- Could this problem happen to others? If so, how do I alert them?
- Does this problem affect others? How? What can be done?

Taking the time to reflect on problems may help you and others in your organization learn from your experiences.

Project Manager's Checklist for Chapter 9

❑ Project control does *not* mean dictating to team members how to perform their activities or roles.

❑ The project control process should focus on gathering and analyzing information that will optimize decision-making.

❑ The project manager must gather information and insight on the past, present, and future when making decisions on guiding the course of the project.

❑ Essential to the information-gathering process is free, open, and honest communication between members of the project team and the project leader.

❑ Corrective action should resolve problems in a way that minimizes losses to project targets (schedule, cost, functionality, and quality) at the lowest additional risk.

❑ Decisions on corrective action should be influenced by the preferences of stakeholders. Try to determine which targets—schedule, cost, functionality, or quality—are most important to them.

Managing the Project Interfaces

B rad had not been a project manager very long before he realized that he wasn't functioning in a vacuum. And as we've continually discovered through our observations of Brad, there are *many* interfaces between him and his surroundings and between Project Apex and its "surroundings." Some are people; some aren't. In some cases, the interfaces are obvious; in other cases, they're not so obvious. What Brad has quickly come to realize, though, is that nearly every interface has the ability to affect him and his project—some of them significantly.

You will be in exactly the same situation with your project. One of the most important things you can do as a project manager is recognize that interfaces are a big part of project life. Your project—just like Project Apex—will not exist in a vacuum. And, of course, just like Brad, neither will you as the project manager.

Some interfaces you'll encounter may be capable of exerting more influence on your project than even you and your team can—if you don't handle them properly. Learning how to recognize and properly deal with them can have a profound effect on the success of your project and on your level of heartburn.

As we're about to learn, it's unlikely that you'll have much *control* over interfaces. But you can identify them, learn to understand them, work with them, and adapt to them. In short, you can *manage* them.

This chapter will help you do that effectively.

What Are "Project Interfaces"?

Consider for a minute that you and your project are at the center of things. Any experience as a project manager will tell you that this view of the world is far from reality! But it allows a good perspective on project interfaces. Figure 10-1 shows some of the typical points where you and your project are in contact with the outside world.

Note that some of the interfaces in Figure 10-1 are people. The people who interface with you and your project are usually

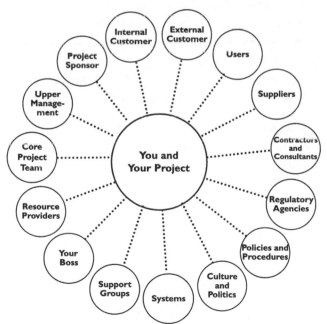

Figure 10-1. A project manager's interfaces

called *stakeholders*. Technically, stakeholders can be something other than people (a department, for example), but I've found it easy to consider stakeholders simply as the "people" component of project interfaces. Let's examine who these people are and what makes them so important to us.

What Makes a Stakeholder a Stakeholder?

"Stakeholder" is an extremely common term in project management. Although you'll find a wide variety of definitions for the term, one of the best ways of defining it is to consider *what makes a stakeholder a stakeholder*. What exactly are the characteristics of stakeholders and stakeholder groups? Several of the most widely accepted ones are listed below. It's important to note that any *one* of these characteristics can make someone a stakeholder:

- Stands to gain or lose through the success or failure of the project
- Provides funding for the project
- Has invested resources in the project
- Participates in (works on) the project
- Is affected by the outputs of the project
- Is affected by the outcome of the project
- Is in the "chain of accountability"

All of these characteristics are probably clear, except perhaps the *chain of accountability*. This term relates to an interesting twist on the ordinary interpretation of "stakeholder" and is worth mentioning for its political implication. The chain of accountability is often seen within complex matrix organizations, where a number of departments exist, each with layers of management. In organizations structured this way, several signatures must often be secured before a project is finally considered approved. Everyone who signs off to approve the project is viewed as taking on some accountability for the project. These people are in the *chain of accountability*. As such, they may see themselves as stakeholders—and feel that they have the right to exert influence on the project, if they sense the need.

Politically astute project managers will pay close attention to who these people are.

What Do You Need to Know About Stakeholders?

As we'll soon see, stakeholders can be in any department or at any level within the organization. You'll constantly be interfacing with stakeholders throughout the life of your project. This leads us to another critical consideration: what do you need to know about stakeholders to properly manage your relationship with them? Here some of the key things you should try to learn about project stakeholders:

Who They Are (by Name). Make sure you know who each stakeholder is—*by name.* Don't be content to recognize that classes of people (such as functional supervisors) are stakeholders. Figure out every individual stakeholder.

The Nature of Their Stake. What do they stand to gain if you succeed—or lose if you fail? How much? In what way? Does the outcome of the project affect them professionally or personally?

What They Expect from You. You can best find out what they expect by meeting with stakeholders individually. Since this is time-consuming, you may want to limit face-to-face meetings to key stakeholders, such as clients or management sponsors. If there are differences between what they expect and what you believe they should reasonably expect, you'd better work those differences out as soon as possible.

What You Expect from Them. This is, of course, the flip side of the previous item. However, some project managers have difficulty expressing their expectations to members of management. If you feel this way, bear in mind that stating expectations does *not* mean that you're telling them what to do or how to act. If you express your expectations of management correctly, it should seem more like a description of the support you need than a prescription for their behavior.

Their Priorities. In this case, the term "priorities" refers to the four major elements of success and control that we discussed

Smart Managing

Get to Know Them

The more you know about stakeholders, the better your chances for developing and maintaining a strong and beneficial relationship with them. Cultivating good relationships with stakeholders may help you in ways you can't envision at the outset of the project.

earlier in the book: schedule, cost, performance, and quality. As mentioned previously, try to gain an understanding of which of these elements is most important to key stakeholders, such as the client and management sponsor.

The Rules of Engagement. This item pertains primarily to the process of communication and, in particular, your personal interaction with a given stakeholder. It's probably most relevant to your interaction with members of management. For example, consider what type of communication a given manager may prefer—formal written or informal oral. In other words, would they prefer that you phone them and follow with a memo or write them a memo and follow with a phone call? In some cases, these are not trivial issues.

Whether They Are Friend or Foe. Is a given stakeholder likely to support you and your project—or more apt to undermine your efforts? The answer to this question is normally related to the *nature of the person's stake.*

Internal Stakeholders and Their Roles

Let's begin our examination of stakeholder groups with internal stakeholders—people within your organization. One of the things that make internal stakeholders particularly important is that the *perceived* success of your project is often judged by the perceived satisfaction of internal stakeholders. Even if you meet the prescribed project targets and run the project efficiently, if certain internal stakeholders form an unfavorable opinion of your project, your image will still suffer. In addition, most of the key decision makers are internal stakeholders.

Let's look at some of the key stakeholder groups—who they

are, your relationship to them, and how they can affect you and your project.

The Internal Customer

Customers are ordinarily the people for whom you're doing the project. Internal customers are normally people within your company who have a particular need that your project will address. The internal customer often pays for the project and receives the benefits (business impact) and/or project deliverables. Project Apex is an example of an internal project: the manufacturing and assembly department that Brad has been interfacing with is his internal customer.

The Project Sponsor

"Project sponsor" is not ordinarily a specific organizational position; it's a role played on projects. A sponsor is typically a representative of upper management who's personally involved in the project. In many cases, it's a person with a very high stake in the project outcome. It can be particularly valuable to have a project sponsor when you face problems, issues, or situations that lie beyond your sphere of influence. In short, they can help you when you don't have the connections or the clout to make things happen. Sponsors may facilitate approvals or decisions, assist with resource assignments (or reassignments!), and serve as advisors and mentors to you as you manage the project. A good sponsor will also help you overcome political and organizational obstacles. Make sure that you keep your sponsor fully informed about your project.

Go Out and Get One if You Have To!

Smart Managing

A project sponsor can be an invaluable asset to you and your project—particularly if you work in a matrix environment and your project is large or complex. If a sponsor is not formally identified, *go out and get one!* Seek out a member of management who has a relatively high stake in the success or failure of your project. Ask if he or she is willing to serve as the project sponsor. Be prepared to describe the role and your expectations, if they ask. Many times, you will find them to be quite willing; after all, they *want* you to succeed.

Upper Management

The senior management of your organization may or may not be involved in your project in a direct way, but they're the ultimate stakeholders. What if all of your organization's projects were dismal failures, wasting large amounts of money and other resources for little or no business results? Upper management would be perceived as incompetent. If you're assigned to a critical or high-visibility project, upper management may wish to play a more active role. Hopefully, their involvement will be positive and not lead to unnecessary or unproductive meddling or micromanagement—two of the project manager's greatest fears.

The Core Project Team

Many people will work on your project, perhaps dozens if your project is large. In many cases, however, you'll be directly and immediately assisted by a relatively small group of people—the *core team*. Core teams can be constructed any number of ways. In most matrix organizations, various departments or work groups will be needed to complete the project. In this kind of project environment, core teams are normally composed of a *single* representative from each participating department.

When a clear-cut departmental model is not appropriate, core team roles often tie more closely to the work to be done. As major elements of work are identified, shrewd project managers will seek out the person who's best equipped to perform that element of work effectively and efficiently.

Functional Supervision (Resource Providers)

In matrix organizations, it's common for project managers to "borrow" resources from other departments. The managers who control those resources are a special kind of stakeholder. When their people are working on your projects, they're representing their department. You might think that this kind of relationship would foster a strong sense of stake within functional supervisors. Unfortunately, that's not always the case. Gently reminding functional supervisors that the people they assign are a reflection on them and their group can help build a stronger sense of

> ### Strive for Single-Point Accountability
> **TRICKS OF THE TRADE**
>
> In multi-disciplined environments, several people from each of several departments may end up working on your project. In situations like this, you should try to assemble a core team that consists of a single representative from each participating department or work group. Ideally, this person will assume responsibility for coordinating the work that's executed by his or her department. This "single-point accountability" reduces the number of interfaces you must maintain, you'll always know who to contact, and you greatly reduce or even eliminate the "finger pointing" that can come with dual responsibility.

stake. A bigger concern, though, is the *long-term relationship* you maintain with resource providers. If your relationship is good, you may be able to acquire better resources. It's in your best interest to cultivate and maintain a good relationship with resource providers.

Your Manager (or "Boss")

Nearly all project managers report to someone. Though the concept of a "boss" is in a state of transition, let's use the term here, for simplicity. Even though your boss may not be directly involved in your project, he or she is still a stakeholder. Take Brad, for example, and his boss, Susan. If Brad manages Project Apex poorly, it will reflect poorly upon Susan, because she assigned him as the project manager. More important, Brad, as project manager, is acting as an *agent* of Susan. That's still the way most organizational hierarchies are interpreted—and it's a key issue that you need to appreciate. Your boss, therefore, has a *very big* stake in you and your project. So, you have certain responsibilities. One of the biggest is to keep your boss fully informed at all times. Your boss will view one of your primary responsibilities as protecting him or her from being blindsided—hit by any surprises or lacking some critical information that he or she should have known.

Support Groups

Various groups within your organization—such as legal, accounting, data processing, and clerical—will often play a role more supportive than active, depending on the specific needs of

> **CAUTION!**
>
> ### Some Team Members May Not Be "Good Stakeholders"
>
> One word of caution is worth mentioning about team members behaving as *stakeholders*. As discussed in Chapter 2, some organizational cultures don't create a strong sense that *project excellence* is important; they recognize and reward *functional* excellence, not *project* excellence. If this sounds like your organization, it's possible that your core team members may not feel that they have much of a stake in the outcome of the overall project. They know that as long as they do what's expected, they'll be OK. Be attentive to this phenomenon on your team and manage these situations as we discussed in Chapter 2.

your project. This can lead to a difficult decision: should you make supporting groups part of the regular core team or not? This is a tough call. Having a group representative on the core team and attending regular team meetings will promote team cohesion and enhance the "collective intelligence" we discussed in Chapter 5. However, if their role does not call for ongoing, regular involvement, representatives may feel as if you're wasting their time. This is an issue you should discuss with each individual at the outset of the project. Their contribution—whatever its magnitude—is likely to be richer if they participate at a level that you're both comfortable with.

External Stakeholders and Their Roles

By definition, external stakeholders are not part of your organization. Although they normally want your project to succeed, their stake is often focused more inwardly. This is true of most external stakeholders, except those for whom you're doing the project (external customers). Most external groups—particularly those supplying goods and services—are inclined to take a parochial view of your project. This means that you cannot always count on them to put what's best for the project ahead of what's best for them. This may sound cynical, but it's reality.

The External Customer

Projects that address the needs of external customers are typically characterized by contracts, so project managers normally have a clear idea of the customers. Very often, the biggest challenge with external customers is getting them to articulate their needs in a clear and final way. Although unclear objectives may be a problem with internal customers as well, the stakes are higher with external customers because there are contracts—sometimes with fixed dollar amounts. In addition, some external customers have the attitude that because they're paying the bill they have the right to change their minds about what they want. Whether that's philosophically true is irrelevant; the important point is that such a view of the world can make life very difficult for you. So, be attentive and take precautions.

The User

User groups are a special case of external customers, primarily when you're developing or producing a product that's marketed and sold to outside consumers. I like to think of users as *latent stakeholders*. In most cases, they don't realize that they're stakeholders, as they're probably unaware of your project and the products it creates until those products are released into the marketplace. You must often act as a surrogate stakeholder by asking key questions about users' likes and dislikes, preferences and choices, and so forth. The organization's marketing department may play the role of surrogate user, so projects that involve user groups often necessitate maintaining a strong interface with marketing.

> **Get Educated!**
>
> If you believe that you'll be leading many projects that involve external customers, get educated in the legal and contractual aspects of project management. Many good books and training courses cover these subjects.
>
> Smart Managing

Suppliers

Nearly all projects require materials that must be obtained from outside companies. Finding reliable suppliers of high-quality products can be difficult, though. This is one reason why many companies adopt *preferred supplier programs*. Make sure you know whether your company has such a program. In principle, these programs attempt to forge long-term, cost-effective relationships with high-quality suppliers. Unfortunately, however, you cannot always count on quality; preferred suppliers are often determined more by cost than by quality. And you should never simply assume that you can rest easy because you're using a preferred supplier. In fact, you should never get complacent with *any* supplier relationship or agreement. A common mistake made by project managers is assuming that suppliers do not require much of your attention because you have a contract, purchase order, or specifications sheet. You should monitor and control suppliers as much as any other individual or group working on your project.

Contractors and Consultants

Much of what was said about suppliers holds true for contractors and consultants. The main difference is that you're purchasing labor or services instead of materials. However, you should be aware of two big issues with this group of stakeholders.

First, contractors and consultants will probably feel less stake in your project than any of the stakeholder groups. The extent of their stake rarely goes beyond their body of work and their image. After all, protecting their image is vital to their survival. It's unlikely that they would do something that would jeopardize their image—even if it were the right thing to do for your project. Harsh? Yes. Reality? Yes!

Your second concern relates to purchasing services if you aren't familiar with a particular contractor or consultant. Because talk is cheap and glossy brochures are easy to print, you need to be cautious when engaging a contractor or consultant. Whenever possible, try to use performance-based criteria and a verifiable track record when selecting these stakeholders.

Other Interfaces

Most of your interfaces will be stakeholders. However, there are other entities that you will interface with, so you need to be aware of them and know how to manage them.

Regulatory Agencies

Regulatory agencies, such as OSHA and EPA, are not listed here as stakeholders for a very good reason: the people in these agencies couldn't care less whether your project succeeds or not. The extent of their stake is to make sure that you behave as you're supposed to. Many of us tend to want to sidestep any involvement with this interface group. If you do that, you may be taking a large risk. Ordinarily, your best bet is to cooperate with regulatory agencies, as they often assess penalties that far exceed what you may save by trying to avoid them. A common mistake that project managers make with regulatory agencies isn't avoiding them, however—it's simply *forgetting to involve them.* A very important thing to keep in mind with regulatory agencies is that they have one thing that you don't—power. And lots of it.

Organizational Policies and Procedures

This is an important interface. As a project manager, you're expected to follow the policies and procedures of your organization. That's just one of the unspoken expectations of project managers in most organizations. So, you'd better be familiar with the policies and procedures that affect your project.

One dilemma that you're likely to face is whether to abide by the ones that you disagree with. (And it's likely that you *will* disagree with some!) You should not disregard policies for purely personal reasons—it's bad for your image. Very often, the only reason that most people find justifiable for disregarding the rules is when *not* following them is more beneficial to your project. Ensuring the success of your project is seen as your highest duty to the organization.

> **Beware of Non-Human Interfaces** ⚠️ CAUTION!
>
> No, I'm not talking about your boss! Interfaces with no face—such as organizational policies, procedures, culture, and politics—can affect your project at least as much as any human interface.

Systems

There are many organizational systems. Most are process-oriented and computer-based, internal to the organization, put in place to help the organization function more efficiently. Examples include the labor charging and payroll systems, data processing systems, procurement or purchasing systems, inventory-tracking systems, manufacturing systems, and possibly even project management systems in the form of scheduling or cost reporting systems. You need to understand which (if any) of these systems are relevant to your project. As with policies and procedures, you're ordinarily expected to use the systems in which your organization has invested so much money.

Culture and Politics

This interface has been mentioned many times throughout this book—for good reason. A project manager who does not understand or chooses to discount the impact that the organizational culture or political environment may have on the project is destined to a life of mediocrity at best. You need to be aware of cultural and political elements and seek to understand them. The following questions may help:

- How do various groups feel about project management?
- Who are the real decision-makers in any given situation?
- What kind of results tends to get positive recognition and rewards?
- Why do these two departments hate one another?
- Which members of management can make things happen and which just blow hot air?
- What can I get away with?
- What types of behaviors and attitudes are valued around here?

Being politically astute is not the same as "sucking up." It means such things as knowing who to see in case of trouble, knowing the boundaries of appropriate risk-taking, figuring out who will support you and who won't, and keeping key players informed.

Special Considerations in Interface Management

In addition to identifying, understanding, and properly handling specific interfaces, there are a few special issues you should consider with regard to interfaces.

Managing the Management Interface

It probably goes without saying that this particular interface is important to your future. The way you deal with organizational management forms the basis of their impressions of you and your potential for advancement within the organization.

Interfacing with managers—upper management in particular—can be challenging at times. They'll continually provide input, direction, and feedback throughout the project. Unfortunately, not all of those managers will consider your personal and interpersonal needs as carefully as you consider the needs of those you direct. Consequently, you may receive input, feedback, and direction:

- When you aren't expecting it
- In a form you may not comprehend
- That you do not agree with or you feel is in error
- With little explanation or justification
- Without concern for your buy-in or commitment
- Without regard for your feelings or self-esteem
- That you may find personally or professionally offensive

What can you do in negative situations like this? You must maintain control at all times, while ensuring that communication channels are clear and concise.

The box on the next page offers some general suggestions for dealing with these kinds of negative interactions—and a couple of positive ones. As is true with situational leadership, your ability to vary your style and react appropriately is vital to maintaining a healthy long-term relationship with the management interface.

Developing Mutual Expectations

One of the most beneficial and yet neglected activities in project work is taking the time to clarify mutual expectations with stakeholders. Many people assume that they'll automatically know what all of the other parties are going to do, how they'll behave, and what they'll deliver. Yet I've witnessed countless situations

> **When reacting to negative feedback:**
> 1. Ask for clarification on anything you don't understand.
> 2. Don't bluff; admit if you don't know the answer.
> 3. Don't lie.
> 3. Don't blame the situation on other people or circumstances.
> 4. Don't promise anything you know you can't deliver.
> 5. Correct misconceptions tactfully.
> 6. Confirm your intention to investigate any complaints.
> 7. Don't react emotionally.
>
> **When reacting to positive feedback:**
> 1. Share praise liberally.
> 2. Don't be too self-effacing ("really, it was nothing", "I guess I lucked out").

where the project ends and one or both parties are disappointed.

When expectations are not clarified, the results can be finger pointing, rework, poor working relationships, misunderstandings, and feelings of dissatisfaction.

Figure 10-2 lists several examples of basic expectations between a project manager and four stakeholder groups. Use these as starting points for discussions with specific stakeholders on your next project. Then work with stakeholders to expand each list to include more project-specific expectations.

A Customer usually expects the Project Manager to:	The Project Manager usually expects a Customer to:
• Understand the customer's business	• Always speak in terms of needs, not solutions
• Understand the customer's priorities (cost/schedule/quality/performance)	• Articulate requirements in the process as early as possible
• Be capable of looking at things from the "customer's perspective"	• Actively participate in requirements process
• Keep the customer fully informed of progress and changes	• Provide information, data, and insight necessary to do the job
	• Minimize changes during the project

Figure 10-2. Mutual expectations

Upper Management usually expects the Project Manager to:	The Project Manager usually expects Upper Management to:
• Assume total accountability for success of the project • Abide by the limits of authority and control that have been granted to the role of Project Manager • Keep them fully informed of project status and changes through informative, concise reports • Alert them as soon as it becomes evident that any prescribed project targets cannot be met	• Define expectations, including project and individual performance, limits of authority and autonomy, etc. • Set reasonable and achievable targets and goals • Openly and formally affirm support for project to all appropriate managers and organizational members • Arbitrate/resolve counterproductive political infighting
Functional Supervisors usually expect the Project Manager to:	**The Project Manager usually expects Functional Supervisors to:**
• Articulate resource needs clearly and in enough time to react • Be sensitive to people's duties outside the project • Provide appropriate growth opportunities for their people • Keep them informed of project status and changes	• Supply the "right" talent for the job • Minimize project disruptions through continual reassignments • Keep their people's knowledge at a "state-of-the-art" level • Promote project-oriented mentality (discourage silo thinking)
The Project Manager's boss *usually* **expects the Project Manager to:**	**The Project Manager usually expects his/her boss to:**
• Involve him/her in appropriate aspects of project • Develop a regular project status-reporting format and frequency that meets his or her needs • Keep him/her fully informed proactively • Protect his/her from getting "blindsided"	• Support him/her in the face of problems • Help negotiate politically oriented issues, particularly high-level or organizationally sensitive ones • Serve as a spokesperson for his/her project to upper management

Figure 10-2 Continued

Understanding Authority and Influence

One of the aspects of project leadership for which many project managers develop a natural appreciation is their *position of power* relative to each individual stakeholder. Project managers get things done and make things happen *through others*. When working with someone to produce a particular outcome, you will find yourself in one of two basic power positions. Let's examine these two positions and how they relate to your life as a project manager.

Position #1: Authority. If you're in a position of authority, you have the ability to produce a preferred outcome alone. Very simply, you can get what you want. This situation is common in the military, but rare for project leaders. In numerous organizations, however, project managers are perceived as having a small amount of *implied authority* over team members and some support groups. The amount of perceived authority is often related to how the organization defines the role of the project manager and the level of support project managers tend to receive from organizational management. Even if you sense that you have this implied authority, it's ordinarily not wise to use it very often, as this can often lead to feelings of resentment.

Some project managers are also "granted" some implied authority by team members and others through a phenomenon referred to as *expert power*. People believe in them because they have special technical, administrative, or people skills and knowledge.

> **Key Term**
>
> **Expert power** The ability to gain support through superior knowledge or capability. In other words, people are more willing to do what you ask because they feel you know what you're doing.

Position #2: Influence. Influence means that you *work with others* to produce desired outcomes. Influence is most often used when dealing with people who do not report to you and is a very common power, particularly in matrix organizations. In this situation, you're perceived as being on the same level of power. Project leaders get most things done through this method.

Project Manager's Checklist for Chapter 10

❑ Your project exists within an environment that includes many points of interface.

❑ Any one of a number of characteristics can make someone a stakeholder in your project. There may be many more stakeholders than you might think.

❑ You need to actively manage stakeholder relationships.

❑ Learn as much as you can about every stakeholder. This will help you manage your relationship with them more effectively.

❑ Project sponsors can be extremely helpful. Go out and find one if one doesn't come to you.

❑ Beware of external suppliers, subcontractors, and consultants; typically, they don't assume a particularly strong sense of stake in the outcome of your project.

❑ Non-people interfaces—such as policies, procedures, organizational culture, and politics—are key interfaces, just as important and influential as the people interfaces.

Project Communication and Documentation

While managing Project Apex, Brad has been constantly communicating with others in and around his project. This is not uncommon. In fact, according to some estimates, you can expect to spend more than 80% of your time communicating in some way. You'd better know how to do it well!

There are many approaches you can take in communicating and many media to choose from. No matter what approach or media you choose, communicating effectively requires significant skill. We'll explore these and other aspects of communication in this chapter.

We'll also take a look at documentation, which many project managers dislike immensely and consider an administrative burden. Admittedly, it can require substantial effort, but if done properly documentation can be much more of a friend than foe. One of the keys to managing documentation effectively is to avoid excess—to do only what makes sense and adds value. So in this chapter, we'll limit our examination to the documents viewed as most critical to successful project management.

Communication and documentation are a natural combination. They bind the project together from start to finish, as the backbone of sound project management.

Both are surprisingly difficult to do well without experience—and some preparation. In my experience, one of the things that separates effective project managers from relatively ineffective ones is how much *forethought* (dare I say planning?) they put into communication and documentation from the very beginning of their project. This chapter is intended to help you plan and execute communication and documentation effectively.

The Project Management Configuration Plan: A Documentation and Communication "Road Map"

Even if your organization has documented project management procedures, it's likely that they're not overly detailed. Even worse, your organization may have no formalized procedures whatsoever. Either of these situations is likely to severely hamper your ability to achieve project success.

To reduce confusion and increase control, you should consider preparing specific guidelines around project management procedures for every project you manage. I like to refer to this set of guidelines as the Project Management Configuration Plan—or PMCP. (Note: this is my term, as there's no industry standard term for this.) The PMCP is really a description of how you intend to "conduct business" from a project management standpoint. It is an excellent marriage of communication and documentation—and an excellent way to communicate your expectations.

A well-designed PMCP will address these (and many other) questions:

Who should be involved in project planning?
- What's the preferred scheduling approach?
- What approach should be used in preparing cost and schedule estimates?
- What planning documents are expected to be produced?

- How will work assignments be made?
- What are appropriate and inappropriate channels of communication?
- What will be the frequency of team meetings?
- How will progress be tracked?
- What documentation will be used for change control?

Figure 11-1 lists some of the elements you'll need to include in your Project Management Configuration Plan. As with any other template or form, you'll need to expand or modify the PMCP to suit your specific project, your organizational culture, the members of your project team, your organization's existing procedures, and your management style.

The PMCP serves as an excellent communication tool. It provides several stakeholders (your team, the customer, and

Planning	**Execution and Control**
General approach	*Progress measurement*
• preferred process	• methods of measuring
• who should be involved	• verification requirements
• required documentation	• required documentation
Scope definition	*Change management procedures*
• defining tasks	• when to report a change
• sizing of work packages	• required documentation
• use of a WBS dictionary	• approval limits and procedure
Time estimating	dure
• estimating effort	• distribution of contingency
• estimating duration	*Team meeting guidelines*
• estimating contingency	• frequency
• preparing a basis of estimate	• attendance expectations
Cost estimating	• general agenda
• preferred procedure	• format for status reports
• estimating contingency	
• preparing a basis of estimate	**Communications/Personnel**
Schedule preparation	*Roles and responsibilities*
• graphical format	*Rules of engagement*
• use of software	*Mutual expectations*
	Review and approval procedures

Figure 11-1. Portion of a project management configuration plan

your project sponsor, for example) with a wealth of information regarding how you plan on managing your project.

Methods of Communicating

The way you communicate a message can often be just as important as the

> **Include Existing Procedures**   *Smart Managing*
>
> Any project management procedures that already exist in your organization should be included as part of your Project Management Configuration Plan. Reference them somewhere within your PMCP and make certain that the members of your team are familiar with how to follow them.

message itself. For example, consider how many times you've received a phone call or a note from someone that pertained to a very important issue. After reading the note or hanging up the phone, you reacted by thinking, "They didn't bother to tell me in person." If you're like me, that reaction probably altered your perception of the message in some way—and of the person who sent it, perhaps.

As a project manager, you must consider this aspect of communication. Like it or not, you're under constant scrutiny from people who are forming impressions of you, your approach, and your intentions. The way you communicate is likely to influence their impressions of you as much as any other single thing you do. You have a variety of choices for communicating with others; choosing the best way to communicate in a particular situation is a very important decision. Some choices relate to approach and style, while others relate to the medium you choose. Let's examine some considerations around each.

What's the Best Communication Approach?

No matter which medium you use to communicate, your basic approach can affect the way your message is received and interpreted. As in the example above, a phone conversation, a note, and a personal visit were all effective ways to transmit *message content.* The choice to not communicate in person, however, altered your *interpretation* of the message. Before choosing the best medium, you should consider what would be the best approach. Here are some basic choices.

Face to Face or "Remote"? Obviously, delivering a message in person sends a signal: it may suggest a greater urgency to the message or a higher level of concern or consideration for the recipient. It may also be helpful if an immediate dialogue is expected to ensue. Finally, face-to-face communication affords you the opportunity to observe body language and other nonverbal communication.

> **Key Term**
>
> **Nonverbal communication** Transmitting messages (communicating) without using words. Nonverbal communication can happen through body position and movement, posture, facial expressions, clothing, behavior, and other ways. Nonverbal messages have the ability to replace, emphasize, or contradict verbal messages.

Written or Oral? There are advantages and disadvantages to each of these approaches. The best choice depends on your needs. Preparing a written message affords you the opportunity to rework the message until you feel it's right; however, text messages are subject to misinterpretation because tone, inflection, and feeling are difficult to convey in writing. Verbal communication allows for more immediate back-and-forth communication; with that immediacy, however, comes the risk of saying the wrong things or saying things wrong.

Formal or Informal? Your level of formality may also send a signal. Formal communications may suggest a lack of familiarity, comfort, or friendliness with the other party. If you move from formal toward informal, you're often suggesting that you feel (or would like to feel) that your relationship with the recipient is "warming." Formal communications also send a signal that the content of the message is *official*—that you wish the dealings in question to be open, aboveboard, and not subject to manipulation of any kind. Most contractual dealings are relatively formal.

Advanced Preparation or Impromptu? This issue is most relevant in face-to-face communication. If a situation requires thoughtful input, it may be best to make arrangements in advance, so both parties are aware of the subject and the timing of the communication. A person who is taken by surprise may provide inappropriate or low-quality responses. Unfortunately, setting up a communication session in advance takes time. Impromptu communications may provide a more candid response or offer the opportunity to observe a reaction.

In a Group Setting or One on One? Delivering messages to groups has two advantages: it's efficient and it ensures that everyone hears exactly the same message delivered in exactly the same manner. An obvious exception to this approach occurs when there is some sensitivity to the message, such as situations where some members are personally affected or when proprietary information should not be shared with everyone.

What's the Best Communication Medium?

Considering which basic approach will work best in a given situation can help guide you in determining the best medium of communication. Again, the choices are plentiful. Let's look at some of these methods and a few considerations.

E-mail. The use of electronic mail continues to skyrocket. Some contend that e-mail is an overused (and sometimes inappropriately used) medium. It's certainly convenient—at least for most people. And it ordinarily reaches widely dispersed and distant recipients quickly—although there's no guarantee that the recipient will read the message right away. It auto-

> **Make Sure You "cc" the Right People on Your E-mail Note**
>
> **TRICKS OF THE TRADE**
>
> Thanking someone for a job well done via e-mail can seem a bit impersonal. However, making sure that the right people are included on your "cc" list can change all that. Copying a team member's supervisor on a note of congratulations or thanks is a powerful, effective, and easy way to provide recognition and positive visibility.

matically provides a permanent record for the sender and receiver (which may be good *or* bad). Also, as with any written message, e-mail messages are subject to misinterpretation.

And the ease with which e-mail notes may be forwarded to other parties forces you to be careful about what you put in the message and how you word it. All in all, e-mail is a convenient and effective method of communicating, if used properly.

Telephone. Calling someone on the phone can be an immediate (if they answer!), interactive method of communicating without creating a permanent, written record. Phone conversations allow you to hear voice inflections, although obviously you cannot view body language or other nonverbal communication. Although an upbeat phone call is considered "warmer" than a written note, it doesn't have the same effect as a personal visit or any other face-to-face interaction. (The same holds true for unpleasant interactions.) Unanticipated phone calls are subject to the same shortcomings or advantages of impromptu communications.

Voice Mail. When people don't answer their phone, you can often rely on voice mail. This may create issues for you, if you're not careful. When you place a call, you're often expecting a dialogue. If you're forced to use voice mail, you must immediately convert your message to a monologue, which doesn't always come out sounding as you'd like it: the message can become awkward or confusing for the recipient. And, as with e-mail, there's no guarantee that the message will be received in a timely manner.

> **MISTAKE PROOFING**
>
> ### Prepare for Your Recording Session
>
> If you're anything like me, you've left some strange and curious voice messages for people. Why? Because you fully expect to reach the person you're calling—and are surprised to get voice mail. The result can sometimes be a confusing "dialogue" with someone who isn't there. This can lead to misunderstandings. Whenever you phone someone, think about what you intend to say and how you can say it in case you get voice mail.

Handwritten Notes. Probably the most informal of all communication methods, short notes written by hand are an excellent way to provide positive recognition. Although they usually take very little effort, they convey "the personal touch" much more than verbal approaches or formal memos or e-mail messages. Among the drawbacks of these types of notes is that they're geographically limited.

Printed and Mailed Memos and Letters. With the advent of e-mail, memos and letters are now generally reserved for more formal or official communication. They're slow and one-sided, but good when formal signatures are required and a permanent record is desired. Hence, printed, mailed memos and letters are still used frequently in contractual situations.

Informal Visits. A visit is ordinarily an informal and personal way to maintain communications with an individual. Although you may not be carrying a specific message, an informal visit can often lead to a more valuable or productive communication session than you might get from a formal one-on-one or a group meeting. Informal visits are also appropriate when confidential, personal, or sensitive subjects need to be covered.

Formal Presentations. Formal presentations are often used in situations where the distribution of information may be enhanced by an explanation or the information is too complex for written documentation. Formal presentations are often done in a group setting, thus ensuring that everyone gets the same level of understanding. They allow for impressive graphical displays of information, but often require a lot of preparation. They're effective when you're trying to promote understanding, enlist support, or expedite a decision (e.g., management approval to proceed). However, formal presentations can be challenging or risky, as you rarely have control over the entire session. And, if poorly done, they may do more harm than good.

Remote Updating Through Project Management Software. This method of communicating is unique to project management. One of the newer features that some project management software companies are promoting is the ability for team members to provide project status to the project manager without any need to meet face to face. Although this communication method may be a boon for geographically dispersed teams, the software manufacturers fail to make that distinction. This leaves some project managers believing that it's better to get electronic updates from team members just down the hall than to meet with them regularly. I disagree and would not recommend that you let this electronic marvel replace your opportunity to look team members in the eye and ask them how they're coming along on their activity.

General Guidelines for Effective Communication

Choosing the right approach and the best medium are critical decisions. But how do you actually go about the process of communicating? This may seem like overkill to some, but not taking the time to plan and failing to follow some basic guidelines can lead to disastrous results. Whenever you're communicating with others—face to face, in writing, by phone, or through memos—keep in mind these guidelines for effective communication:

Consider the function of the communication. Think about the purpose of your communication. For example, are you trying to provide information, offer an opinion, gain support, or drive a decision? This will have an effect on how you structure the communication and what approach may be best.

Get to the point. I've been subjected to countless phone calls and memos that took far too long to get to the reason for the communication. Don't do that to others. Strive to be concise.

Apply what you learned in English class. Pay attention to spelling, grammar, sentence structure, and composition when communicating—particularly in written communication.

Avoid distractions. Consider everything that may distract the recipient from getting the full impact of the communication and strive to reduce or eliminate them. Choose the right timing and physical setting. Make sure that your conduct isn't distracting.

Consider long-term effects. We often think of communication as being immediate and short-lived. However, that's not always the case. What if your e-mail note gets forwarded to the wrong person? What if you fail to include someone in a critical communication? Such matters may have long-term implications. Think about this when you're planning your communication.

Follow up. It's often good practice to follow up on your communications. Did the person receive the message? Did they understand it? Do they have any questions?

Conducting High-Quality Meetings

Meetings can be a very effective way to conduct business. They bring people together for a relatively short amount of time so that large amounts of information can be shared. As mentioned several times previously, you should conduct core team meetings regularly to promote a steady flow of information to and from team members. But you'll find that there are many other times when you may need to call for a meeting. Meetings are a critical form of communication.

Unfortunately, many people view meetings unfavorably, in part because they feel that there are too many meetings and most are poorly run, so it can be a struggle to get people to attend. If you develop a reputation for running effective, no-nonsense meetings, you increase your chances of consistently getting team members there to conduct business. Understanding *when to call a meeting* and learning *how to run one* are key skills that do not get sufficient attention in many organizations. Here are some tips about calling and conducting meetings— core team meetings as well as general meetings.

Determine whether a meeting is even required. You can avoid being viewed as "meeting-happy" if you follow these basic guidelines:

- Don't call a meeting if a series of phone calls will serve the purpose.
- Don't call a meeting to decide something that you can or should decide.
- Don't call regular team meetings any more frequently than necessary.
- Don't call a meeting if you're reasonably certain there's nothing new to discuss.
- Don't prolong a meeting if the group is through conducting the business at hand.

Be clear on the purpose of the meeting. Being clear on the objective of the meeting will sharpen its focus and therefore improve efficiency. Here are the basic meeting types and their purpose:

- *Progress*—to assess status and accomplishments and to set more goals
- *Decision*—to develop and agree upon a decision
- *Agreement*—to present a case on a decision and seek collective acceptance
- *Information*—to communicate information or decisions that have been made
- *Opinion*—to collect viewpoints and perspectives from participants
- *Instruction*— to provide direction, enhance knowledge, or teach a skill
- *Review*—to analyze some aspect of the project, such as design

Conduct all meetings in an organized and systematic manner. Consider the following guidelines for conducting effective and efficient meetings:

(A) Prepare for the meeting.
1. Determine the objective or purpose.
2. Prepare introductory comments.
3. Prepare an outline of topics to present or discuss.

4. Determine appropriate meeting duration.
5. Invite the right individuals (the minimum required to accomplish objective).
6. Tell participants how they need to prepare for the meeting.
7. Notify participants in time to prepare; distribute the necessary materials.

(B) Personally and visibly kick off the meeting.
1. State the purpose of the meeting.
2. Review the background, *if necessary.*
3. Announce the specific topics or problems to be discussed.
4. Make sure everyone fully understands the topics or problems.

(C) Ensure attention and participation.
1. Encourage participation; allow everyone to contribute.
2. Control discussion; drive out hostility; prevent monopolization by one person.
3. *Keep the discussion relevant to the meeting purpose!*
4. *Keep things moving forward!*
5. Ensure that participants are fully understanding what's going on.

(D) Close the meeting.
1. *Stick to the allotted time!*
2. Summarize by emphasizing what's been accomplished.
3. Drive to development of an action plan if future work is needed.
4. Clearly indicate follow-up action required; obtain commitment as needed.

(E) Perform necessary follow-up.
1. Prepare and distribute a record of conclusions or recommendations.
2. *Do not* tell a story of everything that happened in the meeting; be concise.

If you follow these suggestions, people will be more likely to attend your meetings. If people begin skipping meetings—particularly team meetings—information flow and general team communication will be hampered and you'll have to devote much more time gathering information and attempting to correct behaviors.

Communication Skills and the Project Manager

Developing the skills needed to communicate effectively takes time, practice, and feedback. Though there are many ways to structure and list the skills required to be an effective communicator, I've found it more useful to think in terms of functional competencies or *abilities*. The most successful project managers I've known had the following abilities:

- Ability to express themselves effectively in conversations with organizational management
- Ability to express themselves effectively in conversations with peers and team members
- Ability to express themselves effectively in conversations with subordinates and support personnel
- Ability to speak naturally in front of a large group
- Ability to prepare and deliver formal presentations
- Ability to speak "off the cuff" effectively
- Ability to negotiate
- Ability to write clear and concise notes and memos
- Ability to write technical reports and other technical material
- Ability to listen effectively
- Ability to know when to talk and when to be quiet
- Ability to provide constructive feedback
- Ability to foster open communication
- Ability to correct others tactfully
- Ability to gauge whether a receiver understands a message or not
- Ability to use vocabulary appropriate to the audience
- Ability to interpret nonverbal communication
- Ability to project poise and self-confidence

As you can see from the length of this list (and believe me, I could have listed several more abilities), communication requires many skills. There are many books, articles, and training programs on communicating effectively, but one of the most important ways to improve your skills is to get into the habit of monitoring and critiquing your communication style continuously, asking yourself key questions, such as the following:

In interactive conversations:
- Do I speak clearly and at the right speed?
- Do I enunciate?
- Do I project my voice appropriately (not too loud or too soft)?
- Do I offer others sufficient opportunity to respond?

In oral presentations:
- Do I speak with confidence?
- Do I have any distracting mannerisms?
- Do I offer sufficient opportunity for reactions or questions?
- Do I use media appropriately?

In written correspondence:
- Is my choice of words clear and unambiguous?
- Does the message flow in a way that others can easily follow my train of thought?
- Do I avoid the use of slang and colloquialisms?
- Do I use correct grammar?

If possible, try to find an associate who can provide feedback on your communication skills and style. Because communication is such a difficult challenge, you should never stop trying ways to improve your ability to communicate effectively.

Key Project Documentation

Proper documentation—like communication—is a critical *support function* of project management. And because each project is unique, no specific level of detail is appropriate for all projects. However, there are certain fundamental—or foundational—documents that most project managers will agree are useful.

Several of the documents we'll be reviewing in this chapter have been presented in earlier chapters. What we will do here is provide a framework of understanding about documentation: when certain documents are used, why they are important, and how they relate to one another.

In Chapter 2, we discussed what occurs in each of the four major phases of a project: Initiation, Planning, Execution, and Close-Out. We'll examine common project documents from that same life cycle perspective, considering the documents typically used in each phase.

Initiating Documents

During the first major phase of a project, the *Initiation Phase*, the project is created, defined in a limited way, officially sanctioned, and launched. This phase begins when a problem or opportunity (i.e., a need) is recognized. An appropriate response to the need is determined and described. (This is actually where the project begins.) The major deliverables and the participating work groups are identified. The project team begins to take shape. Issues of feasibility (*can* we do the project?) and justification (*should* we do the project?) are addressed and formal approval to proceed is granted.

Figure 11-2 illustrates the key documents created during project initiation.

Project Requirements Document. This is perhaps the most fundamental document of your project, as this is where project "life" begins. The Project Requirements Document describes and quantifies the fundamental problem to be solved or opportunity to be exploited (the project need). It can be structured any number of ways, but should include the elements described in Chapter 4 ("Preparing the Requirements Document").

- *Voice of the Customer Analysis or Market Analysis.* Voice of the Customer (VoC) refers to the process of capturing

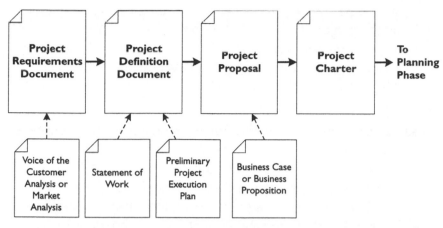

Figure 11-2 Key documents of the project initiation phase

customer or user input. The VoC approach uses interviewing techniques to better understand what the customer wishes and desires or to solicit input on opinions, perceptions, and preferences. Figure 11-3 shows an example of a simple VoC questionnaire. You may or may not choose to use this specific approach. However, the results of *any* meetings or interviews with customers or user groups

What would you like to have in a _____?

What concerns would you like to share?

What comments or recommendations do you have for improvement?

Why did you mention _____?

Why is this _____ important to you?

What does that _____ do for you?

What problems do you have with _____?

What works well about _____?

What doesn't work well about _____?

What would work better than this _____?

What is missing in the _____?

If you were to design/redesign the _____, describe its features, performance, _____, _____.

Figure 11-3. Sample Voice of the Customer questionnaire

should be fully documented and maintained for reference by the project team and other interested parties. In lieu of a VoC analysis, a marketing study may be performed; the key difference is that market analysis doesn't focus on interviewing as the sole source of customer input.

Project Definition Document. The Project Definition Document is essentially a response to the Project Requirements Document. The Project Requirements Document describes a problem; the Project Definition Document describes the solution. It, too, is a foundational project document that can be constructed in various ways. However, it should contain certain specific elements (see Chapter 4, "Preparing the Project Definition Document").

- *Statement of Work.* The Statement of Work is a narrative document that describes the proposed project solution and outlines in limited detail the work to be done. It often includes a listing of major project deliverables, the general approach or methods for doing the work, and how success will be measured. It is the "what" component of the project definition.
- *Preliminary Project Execution Plan.* Just as the Statement of Work describes *what* is to be accomplished, the Preliminary Project Execution Plan describes *how* it is to be accomplished. This precipitates the creation of a Rough Order of Magnitude (ROM) project plan. This is the first version of the plan and typically includes a schedule, cost estimate, preliminary resource plan, and many of the same components that the final project plan will include. The key difference is that preliminary project plans are assumed to be relatively imprecise. As mentioned in Chapter 8, uncertainty is very high at the beginning of your project, so you should try to avoid using precise estimates (see "Using Ranged Values When Expressing Estimated Outcomes").

Project Proposal. It's likely that you'll have to prepare some sort of proposal for management approval. You can construct this proposal in different ways. It should, however, include the elements outlined in Chapter 4 (see "Making a Proposal for Management Approval"). One of the key elements is the business case.

- *Business Case (Economic Analysis).* Many companies prepare a business case or business proposition. (Your organization may have another name for this document.) Ordinarily a key supporting document within the formal management proposal described above, it describes the impact that the project is expected to have on the organization from a business standpoint. Business cases often rely heavily upon an economic analysis as a way to select between competing alternatives and to determine whether a particular project is justifiable from a cost-benefit standpoint. Although you may not be intimately involved in performing the economic analysis, you're likely to be a participant and to be asked for input. Whoever prepares the business case, you should secure a copy, make sure you understand it, and keep it in your project file.

Project Charter/Project Authorization Document. You'll probably have to seek formal management approval before you and your team get into detailed planning. Project Charter is the term commonly used to describe the documentation created to support the formal authorization to proceed with the project.

Planning Documents

In the next major phase of the project, the *Planning Phase*, the project solution is developed in as much detail as possible. It identifies intermediate work products (interim deliverables) and the strategy for producing them. Formulating this strategy begins with defining the required elements of work (tasks) and the optimum sequence for executing them (the schedule). Estimates are made for the time and money needed to perform the work and when the work is to be done. The question of feasibility and justification surfaces again, as formal approval to proceed with the project is ordinarily sought before continuing.

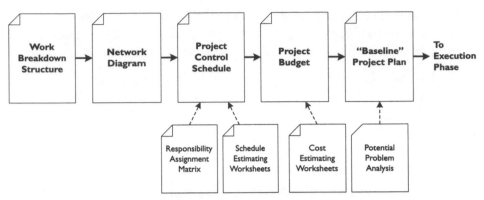

Figure 11-4. Key documents in the project planning process

Figure 11-4 illustrates the key documents that should be created as part of the planning process.

Work Breakdown Structure. The Work Breakdown Structure (WBS) is perhaps the most foundational planning document; just about every other planning document is an extension of the WBS. The WBS lists and organizes into logical subgroups all of the work (activities) required to execute the project.

Network Diagram. Also called Logic Diagram, the Network Diagram depicts the *sequence* of the activities. It's the natural starting point of the scheduling process and it's a critical document in schedule development.

Project Control Schedule (Gantt Chart). The Project Control Schedule is a time-scaled bar chart. It uses the logic developed in the Network Diagram, considers the length of time it takes to execute individual activities, factors in resource availability, and places everything into calendar time. It's the document of choice for helping the team focus on what needs to be done and when. A Project Control Schedule is used primarily as an internal control document for the project team and some stakeholders. Progress evaluation, variance calculation, and continuous forecasting are all done using the Project Control Schedule.

- *Responsibility Assignment Matrix.* The Responsibility Assignment Matrix (RAM) is a two-axis chart that shows how work is assigned. It correlates specific elements of work with specific task performers.

- *Schedule Estimating Worksheets.* Schedule estimating worksheets are directly related to the *basis of estimate* concept mentioned several times throughout this book. A basis of estimate describes the assumptions and proce- dures used in arriving at any and all estimates you receive from estimators. Schedule estimating worksheets should include the assumptions, calculations, and other informa- tion used to estimate required labor hours and the activity durations you would use to create your Project Control Schedule. You should request copies of these worksheets, place them in your project files, and refer to them when- ever you encounter change.

Project Budget (Costs Estimates). You should prepare a budg- et for each project. You should provide estimates for each activ- ity and for the total project. These estimates become the basis for cost tracking and control.

- *Cost Estimating Worksheets.* Just like schedule estimating worksheets, cost estimating worksheets are also related to the concept of basis of estimate. As the title suggests, cost estimating worksheets would include the assump- tions, calculations, and other information used to estimate the expenditure required to execute each activity included in your overall Project Budget. You should have copies of these worksheets, place them in your project files, and refer to them whenever you encounter change.

"Baseline" Project Plan. As mentioned many times before, the project plan is more than just a schedule. The baseline project plan, in fact, includes all of the other documents shown in Figure 11-4. In this figure, the baseline project plan appears to lead directly into execution. Although this is true from a document flow perspective, the reality is that many organizations require formal management approval before proceeding to project execution. This formal approval is what creates the sense of a "baseline." Referring to this edition as the baseline plan signifies that this is the plan that everyone will work toward, and that this is the plan from which you will measure project variances.

- *Potential Problem Analysis.* Potential Problem Analysis is a risk management technique to identify what may go wrong on your project, so that you can take steps to compensate. Although a PPA can be performed at any time, an excellent time is immediately after creating the project plan. The PPA process normally generates a lot of documentation. You should keep copies of these documents in your project files.

Execution and Control Documents

During the third phase, the *Execution Phase*, the prescribed work is performed. As project manager, you continuously monitor progress and you make and record appropriate adjustments as variances from the original plan. Throughout this phase, the project team remains focused on meeting the objectives developed at the outset of the project.

Figure 11-5 illustrates the key documents that should be created as part of project execution and control.

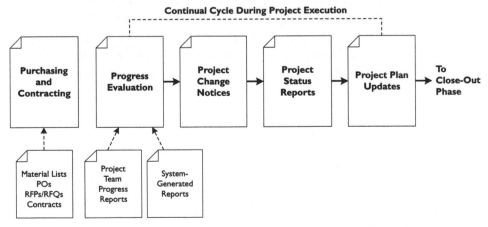

Figure 11-5. Key documents in the process execution phase

Purchasing and Contracting Documents. You'll likely have to procure materials and labor on some or all of your projects. The key documents associated with this process include the following:

- *Material Listing.* Description of materials to be purchased.
- *Purchase Order (PO).* Form used to place orders for materials with outside suppliers
- *Request for Proposals/Request for Quotes (RFPs/RFQs).* Documents used to solicit proposals from prospective vendors of products or services.
- *Contracts.* Legally binding agreements with external suppliers of goods and services

Progress Evaluation. These reports describe the amount of work being accomplished. These documents typically come from two sources:

- *Team-Generated Reports.* This is the information you're collecting in your regular team meetings. You should have documents to serve as a record, such as marked-up schedules or filled-in templates. (See Chapter 9, " How Do You Gather Information?")
- *System-Generated Reports.* If your organization has the capability to store and retrieve project data, such as labor hours or material costs, you should download this data periodically and keep the documents in your project file.

Project Change Notice. There are many names for this critical document, which is used to document and get approval for any significant deviation from the project baseline. At the conclusion of your project, you ought to be able to reconcile the overall deviation between where you ended up and where you told management you'd end up. That reconciliation is embodied in a stack (hopefully short!) of project change notices.

Project Status Report. You should provide regular updates to your organizational management, whether through written reports, one-on-one meetings with the project sponsor, or periodic stand-up presentations.

> **⚠ CAUTION!**
>
> ### Documentation Needs at the Beginning!
>
> All too often, operating, maintenance, service, and other manuals are not considered until the end of the project. This unanticipated work may create an unforeseen expense or a schedule delay. Remember to think about these kinds of documents at the beginning of your project—when you're planning and estimating the project.

Project Plan Updates. The overall project plan should be revised on a regular basis to reflect any changes. As activities are completed and new information about the future becomes available, new forecasts should be prepared.

Close-Out Documents

During the *Close-Out Phase*, the emphasis is on verifying that the project has satisfied or will satisfy the original need. Ideally, the project culminates with a smooth transition from *deliverable creation* (the project) to *deliverable utilization* (the post-project life cycle). The project customer accepts and uses deliverables. Throughout this phase, project resources (the members of the project team) are gradually redeployed. Finally, the project shuts down.

Figure 11-6 illustrates the key documents that should be created as part of project close-out.

Punch List Management. As mentioned in Chapter 2, near the end of your project you're likely to recognize that there are a number of tasks to be completed in order to bring your project

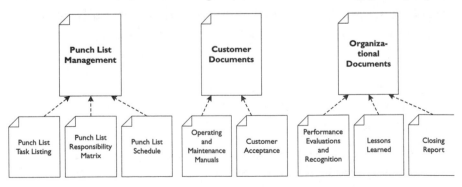

Figure 11-6. Key documents of the project close-out phase

to a successful conclusion. I like to refer to this as the *punch list* (a convenient but unofficial term). It may make sense to create a small plan around the punch list items that would include these documents:

- *Punch List Task Listing.* A simple list of the tasks remaining, which you should review with your customer.
- *Punch List Responsibility Matrix.* A smaller version of the Responsibility Assignment Matrix, showing who's responsible for executing the punch list tasks.
- *Punch List Schedule.* A schedule that includes only the items on the punch list, which you should review with your customer, so as to avoid surprises.

Customer Documents. The key documents related to handing off the project (and project deliverables) to the customer include the following:

- *Operating and Maintenance Manuals.* If your deliverables include equipment that the customer or user is to place into service, you should provide information on how to operate and/or maintain the equipment as part of the original project agreement.
- *Customer Acceptance.* This is a critical document. You should always confirm that the customer is satisfied, is ready and willing to accept the deliverables of the project, and considers the project to be formally concluded.

Organizational Documents. There are a few key documents that are of interest to your organization at the end of the project, including the following three:

- *Performance Evaluations and Recognition.* You may be asked to provide evaluative reports on the performance of team members, generally by the resource providers who assigned the people to your project. You can use this opportunity to formally recognize the efforts of your team members. However, it's often more impressive to create separate documents that can be placed in team members' permanent records.

- *Lessons Learned.* This is a technique to transfer the knowledge gained through your project experiences to the rest of your organization. This can take many forms, but it's often a written report that gets circulated across the entire organization.
- *Closing Report.* Some organizations require a formal report that describes how well the project met its original targets, explains deviations from the plan, and tells whether the benefits promised in the original business case are likely to be realized. For technology-rich projects, the organization often expects technical reports, which describe the project team's experiences in using or creating technology.

Project Manager's Checklist for Chapter 11

❑ Communication and documentation are critical support functions. Think of them as the backbone of strong project management. Top project managers do both effectively.

❑ Prepare a comprehensive list of your communication and documentation expectations at the beginning of your project. Review it in detail with your team.

❑ Communication sometimes requires considerable forethought. When you need to make an important connection with someone, consider the best approach and the best communication medium for the situation.

❑ Don't overlook the value and efficiency of group meetings. And don't underestimate the value of getting a reputation as someone who runs an efficient meeting.

❑ The key to effective documentation is adopting a "fitness for use" mentality. People resent filling out forms and generating paperwork for the sake of feeding the process. Make sure that the documents you request add value to the process.

Bringing Your Project to a Successful Conclusion

B rad's first excursion into the curious world of the project manager has been going fairly well. Sure, there were some rough spots, but all in all, Brad is proud of the job he's done so far. Project Apex is now nearing what he hopes will be a smooth and successful conclusion.

But just when Brad thought he'd be able to kick back and watch Project Apex coast to the finish line, things are beginning to heat up. Attendance at his team meetings has been steadily tapering off. He's having some difficulty getting in touch with some people who were trying to wrap up their last few activities. Brad has been getting questions about what the customer may be expecting, and he can't seem to get any answers.

Actually, Brad is beginning to think that he may be losing his grip a bit. The project plan doesn't seem to be a great deal of help now—at least compared to how much he relied on it throughout project execution. He thinks about calling his unofficial mentor, Ted. He changes his mind, though, feeling that he has probably bothered Ted enough already. Why don't we see what kind of help *we* can give Brad....

Early Termination: Not As Bad as You Think

Before we direct our attention at Brad's situation, let's imagine for a moment that management cancelled Project Apex right in the middle of things. As strange as it may sound, this is a situation that should actually happen more often than it does. There's a good reason why this is true.

In Chapter 2, we discussed how the most fundamental objective of projects is to achieve business results. Actually, it's quite simple—projects are *investments* that your organization makes, from which they expect a return. In real life, investments can sometimes go bad. The same thing can certainly apply to a project. Conditions can change in such a way that the project ceases to become the winner it seemed to be at the outset. Simply stated, management no longer expect the project to have the business impact required to make it wise to keep spending money on it. In many cases, a project such as Apex should be terminated, though in far too many cases, it isn't. There are at least three reasons why early project termination does not occur, even though it should:

Falling Asleep at the Wheel. You should be testing project viability—or financial justification—on a continuous basis throughout the life of the project. Some organizations don't do this very well. Others don't do it at all. Once management approves a project, it simply moves ahead until it's completed. In today's fast-paced and constantly changing environment, it's always possible that there will be changes that undermine the original business case for the project. That means that you need to reconsider the economic viability of every project periodically. And the organization should terminate projects that have lost their business case underpinnings.

Fear of Failure. In many people's minds—and in many of the organizations I am familiar with—early project termination has somehow become linked with *failure*. This couldn't be any further from the truth. Early project termination (for the right business reasons) is actually smart management. It's really just a process of reallocating funds from a relatively poor investment to a relatively good one. I am at a loss to explain why that's viewed as a failure, but I can tell you that I have observed this phenomenon often.

Inertial Pride. Once a project is underway, a certain amount of "inertia" is created by the work that has already gone into a particular project. Pride swells, and a feeling that "we must see this thing through 'til the end" begins to take command of peoples' minds. Unfortunately, it can dull them to a point where judgment is impaired. Even though a team (or organization) senses that a project is on shaky ground, emotional issues such as *not being viewed as quitters*, and *finishing what we started,* seem to become part of the process of determining whether or not to terminate the project. Couple these feelings with the sweat equity that's been invested, and under these circumstances the project is almost certain to continue even when it doesn't make sense any more.

> ### The Earlier the Better
> Normally, there should be no shame in canceling a project that's already underway. The only exception occurs when the project was originally initiated in a flurry of excitement, or was launched for the wrong reason in the beginning, and someone is just now getting around to figuring out that it's a loser. The sooner a bad project is killed, the better—from the standpoint of wasted time, money, and resources, at least. That's why you *should* perform business cases as early in the project life cycle as possible.

Management Challenges at the End of the Project

OK, now back to Brad's situation. As the end of his project draws near, Brad finds himself facing a completely new set of challenges, as you undoubtedly will, as well. These challenges will test your ability to bring the project to a successful conclusion, even if everything has been going well until then. Most of the challenges you'll face will fall into one of three broad categories:

Technical Challenges
- Start-up problems with new products or new designs
- Thorough identification and agreement on all remaining deliverables
- Loss of control of the charges to the project
- Difficulties in securing useful project historical data

Project Team Challenges
- Loss of team functionality as some members complete their tasks
- Loss of interest in tasks such as documentation and "administrivia"
- Attention is diverted as members transition into new projects or other work
- Fear of no future work; hence, foot-dragging

Customer Challenges
- Agreement on what outstanding commitments still exist
- Absence of a clear hand-off strategy
- Change of responsible personnel at critical transition points
- Unavailability of key personnel

Let's examine how to address these challenges by taking a closer look at the *science* of successful project closure, beginning with a list of the key elements.

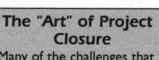

Smart Managing

The "Art" of Project Closure

Many of the challenges that surface at the end of your project will be rooted in behavioral issues. This will test your *leadership* ability. You must remain on the lookout for behavioral cues that will indicate the existence of one or more of these challenges (remember our discussion about the "art of project management"?).

Key Elements of Successful Project Closure

The close-out phase of the project should be given as much or more *project management attention* as any other phase of the project. Bringing a project to a successful conclusion

requires close attention to several different managerial functions. More than any other project phase, project closeout
requires an extremely diverse set of technical, organizational,
and leadership skills. Here are all of the things that you must do
well to maximize your chances of ensuring the successful completion of your project:

Ensure that the project will deliver what was promised.
Actually, this should have been addressed throughout the
entire execution and control phase. As discussed in Chapter 9,
you must continually monitor the functionality and quality of
the project deliverables and protect these from degradation.
From the project closeout perspective, make it your objective
to avoid last-minute surprises.

**Actively lead the project team through a confusing period of
time.** The key term here is *actively*. Make your visibility greater
at this time than at any time since the beginning of the project.
Your project team may begin to disintegrate as a functional unit
when the project nears completion. Communication will
become more difficult for you. You may not be able to count on
a captive audience each week at your team meetings.
Organizing people and things will become increasingly difficult.
All of these issues require that you maintain a high profile and
assume a position of strong leadership.

**Ensure timely completion of the "odds-and-ends" (the punch
list activities).** As mentioned previously, there will come a point
where you can just about abandon the original project plan.
When that happens, you'll find it helpful to focus everyone's
attention on the specific work items required to get the job
done. You handle this through the punch list process described
in the next section of this chapter.

**Prepare for the transition into the next phase in the overall
project life cycle.** As mentioned in Chapter 2, there is ordinarily
an afterlife—at least from the perspective of your project (see
"What Happens 'After the Project' Is More Important than the

Project," page 17). The deliverables your project produces are normally accepted and used by a customer. One of the basic rules of managing projects is that you have the primary responsibility for ensuring that the "handoff" to the customer or user goes smoothly. In fact, don't be surprised if this requires your involvement—on a limited basis, at least—after the traditional completion of the project.

Secure consensus that the project has met the completion criteria. As mentioned previously, you should establish criteria for completion *at the beginning of your project.* If you ignore this issue until the end of your project, disagreements may become significant in scope. Resolving some problems late in the project can involve significant rework.

Obtain customer acceptance and verify customer satisfaction. This is not done enough—at least not in a formalized way. You should strive to create an almost "ceremonial" atmosphere when addressing customer acceptance and customer satisfaction. Just as a formal kickoff meeting communicates project initiation, a formal session where you secure customer satisfaction and acceptance should signal successful project completion in a positive and upbeat way.

Ensure that the project records reflect accurate "as-built" data. This issue may include a wide range of documentation. It refers to the process of updating any and all documents related to your project to reflect the reality that exists at the end of the project. This ensures the existence of accurate historical data, which can be of great value to project teams in the future.

> **Key Term**
> **As-built data** The documentation and information that explains how the project was carried out, valuable for understanding the project management process for future new projects or when this project needs to be taken up again in the future.

Project files (most notably the project plan) should be updated to reflect final "actuals" in terms of cost, schedule, functionality, and quality.

Design documents and specification sheets should be updated to reflect how the deliverables actually look and perform. In many cases, this refers to engineering drawings. Contractual and procurement records should reflect any modifications to agreements or contractual exceptions.

Transfer What You've Learned to Others. The process of performing a "lessons learned analysis" is described below. Whether you perform a full-fledged analysis or simply jot a few notes, it can be important and useful to transfer any critical information you've accumulated or lessons you've learned to anyone who may benefit from your recently acquired wisdom.

Acknowledge the Contribution of Contributors. Acknowledging those who helped you achieve project success is not just a nice thing to do; it's a strong building block for the future—yours as well as the organization's. People who work hard and make significant contributions can actually become de-motivated if their work goes unrecognized. This can hurt the overall effectiveness of the organization. At a more personal level, if you gain a reputation as someone who appreciates a job well done—and you show it— you're more likely to garner the resources you want on your future projects.

> **Show Them That You Care**
> Smart Managing
> Study after study shows that personal recognition means more to people than nearly any other type of reward. Of course financial rewards are nice, but knowing that others appreciate your work is the most meaningful thing to most people. It's a personal affirmation that tells them they matter—something all people crave.

Bring the Project to Efficient Administrative Closure. This may include a wide range of administrative issues. For example, you need to address accounting issues, such as closing open charge account numbers. It also includes ensuring that all outstanding invoices have been submitted, and all bills are paid. It may also include closing out rental or lease agreements, as well as disposing of or storing any leftover materials.

A Few More Words About the Punch List Approach

I first learned about the concept of the punch list while I was having a home built for me. Near the end of my house building experience, it became painfully obvious that there were a number of odds and ends that needed to be done before I would consider the project successfully completed. The painful part stemmed from the fact that my builder was not taking command of the situation and driving these few items to completion. The result was that my satisfaction level was deteriorating on a daily basis—despite the fact that the project had gone well up to that point. A friend of mine suggested that I create a "punch list" of activities, and present it to the builder, suggesting that he get these things taken care of immediately. It worked.

I have since realized that the punch list concept is readily transferable to any kind of project. In fact, you're likely to reach a point on many of your projects where only a few things remain to be done to bring your project to a successful conclusion. Normally, most of these activities will not appear on your original project plan. This is indicative of the loose ends and unexpected issues that often accompany the waning days of a project.

In situations like this, it can be helpful to take a more directive approach. Developing your own punch list, reviewing it with all key stakeholders (most notably the customer), and creating a mini-plan around the punch list is an effective strategy for driving your project to a rapid, organized, and successful conclusion.

> **Key Term**
>
> **Punch list project management** The process of managing all the little things that crop up at the end of a project that have to be done before declaring the project successfully completed. There are nearly always such items, often not anticipated, so it's good to be ready and to know how to handle them, whatever they are.

Figure 12-1 illustrates the process for *punch list project management*. You will undoubtedly notice that this approach is little more than a scaled down version of the planning process introduced earlier in this book.

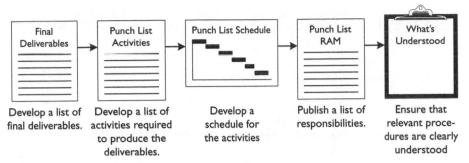

Final Deliverables	Punch List Activities	Punch List Schedule	Punch List RAM	What's Understood
Develop a list of final deliverables.	Develop a list of activities required to produce the deliverables.	Develop a schedule for the activities	Publish a list of responsibilities.	Ensure that relevant procedures are clearly understood

Figure 12-1. Punch list project management

Developing a Project Completion Checklist

The punch list focuses directly on delivery of the main project deliverables. However, you must also be concerned with many other functions involved in project closure. These may include many often overlooked aspects of project delivery as well as the completion of organizational items. To preclude things "falling through the cracks," I'd suggest that you develop a *Project Completion Checklist*.

How to Transfer What You've Learned to Others

One of the ways you can support the ongoing improvement of your organization's project execution methods comes in the form of *lessons learned studies*. The purpose of a lessons learned study is to obtain information through the systematic review of project experiences. Understanding the nature of positive and negative experiences allows future projects to avoid unfavorable influences (problems), and exploit favorable opportunities.

You should include input from all key stakeholders in your study, with you and the project team typically taking a leading role in organizing and carrying out the study. The format and structure of your lessons learned sessions (i.e., the logistics) can vary, but it is often done in a team meeting context, using an approach similar to brainstorming.

Project Completion Checklist

TOOLS The checklist below includes many of the elements listed earlier in this chapter. As with other checklists, you should modify and expand this list to include items specific to your project circumstances.

Customer Issues
❑ Complete all deliverables
❑ Install and test deliverables
❑ Prepare operating manual
❑ Prepare maintenance manual
❑ Train customer's personnel
❑ Agree on level of follow-up support
❑ Conduct formal acceptance review with customer
❑ Verify customer satisfaction

Organizational Issues
❑ Summarize learnings; communicate to the organization
❑ Prepare final technical reports
❑ Evaluate project performance
❑ Conduct final review with management
❑ Prepare project historical files and place in archive

Personnel Issues
❑ Recognize/reward team performance
❑ Write performance evaluations for project team
❑ Assist in reassignment of project personnel

Administrative/Other Issues
❑ Dispose of leftover project material
❑ Close down temporary site operations
❑ Submit final invoices
❑ Forward all final payments
❑ Close out project charge codes and work orders

The Lessons Learned Process

You will probably find the lessons learned process to be most productive when it is oriented toward identifying problems you and your team encountered, and suggesting ways to avoid similar problems in the future. You can accomplish this by asking the following questions for each identified problem:

What was the problem and its impact? Get a description of the perceived problem and its specific effect(s) on the project. In other words, find out what happened to the project as a result of the problem.

What caused this problem to occur? Find out the known or perceived root cause of the problem. If unknown, the cost of securing this knowledge needs to be weighed against its potential benefit.

Why was the problem undetected? This involves a search for possible flaws in monitoring, control, or reporting methods.

> **Root cause** This is the fundamental cause of a problem in a process. Usually a problem occurs in a process because something went wrong in the immediately preceding step or steps. However, this is the not the root cause. The root cause may have been something that happened much earlier and caused a chain reaction that resulted in the problem you're now addressing. Look for the root cause if you want to eliminate the problem permanently.

Caution: This question can also be sensitive, as it may involve individual performance problems.

Can this problem be eliminated in the future? Here you're asking for suggestions on specific steps aimed at precluding a future occurrence. Total elimination is not always possible; however you can come up with strategies for reducing the probability of it happening again.

If it cannot be eliminated, are there ways it could be detected? Here you're looking for suggestions on how the team can alter monitoring, control, or reporting methods in ways that allow for earlier or more reliable detection of the problem.

Tips on Conducting Effective Lessons Learned Studies

In addition to following the process steps outlined above, consider these tips for ensuring a relatively painless and effective experience for everyone involved:

Don't wait until the end of the project to solicit input. Waiting until the last minute to conduct lessons learned studies can be

CAUTION!

Be Sensitive

Inquiring about the cause of a particular problem may be a difficult question to answer in a team context. An individual performance issue, such as neglect, inattention, ignorance, or incompetence may have caused the problem. Try to anticipate and avoid situations where personal embarrassment can occur. Providing an outlet for *anonymous input* is an excellent way to reduce the chances of surfacing sensitive issues in front of the entire group.

problematic. Your team may have partially dissolved, making it difficult to get everyone together. Even if you do get them together, the enthusiasm level may not be what you'd like. Finally, it can be taxing on the memories of those involved, and you may get input that's been altered by the passage of time. Conduct sessions periodically—either at the end of a logical phase of the project, or at some regular interval of team meetings.

Allow the opportunity for submitting input anonymously. As mentioned above, this may allow information and ideas to reach you that are unlikely to surface in group sessions, or would not be appropriate.

Maintain up-to-date and accurate records. This reduces the reliance on people's memories. It will also facilitate the process of determining root causes, verifying the extent of problems, correlating possible causes and effects, etc.

Be sure to examine successes as well as problems. Reviewing positive effects can reinforce the value of certain methods, particularly the ones that people tend to avoidor undervalue.

Tips on Getting Others to Implement Your Lessons

It's one thing to alert others to the problems you faced and to provide information about what you and your team have encountered. However, if you do not structure your information so that others can actually *apply* the lessons you've learned, your organization hasn't really benefited. Below are some suggestions on ensuring that your wisdom is acted on:

Don't relate lessons learned only to the specific context of

your project. Make sure you express lessons learned in general terms in order to benefit the organization at large. Generalize the conclusions from your project's lessons learned in a way that's meaningful to the widest possible audience.

Don't just communicate "what went well" and "what didn't." Unfortunately, some lessons learned studies are little more than a brain dump of *what went well* and *what didn't go well.* A lack of analysis—or synthesis—fails to provide others in the organization with any real "lesson." For others to benefit, they need to know how to avoid the problems or to reduce the impact if the problem occurs.

Include lessons learned reviews as a front-end activity in the project life cycle. Lessons learned studies are traditionally thought of as concluding activities only. This one-dimensional view fails to ensure their application by future project teams. Some organizations have addressed this problem by including a step near the beginning of their project process that obligates project teams to review lessons learned files as part of their up-front planning. This strategy "closes the loop" on the learning cycle and helps to ensure that the team actually applies these lessons.

And So We've Reached the End

Or should we say that Brad has reached the end? When all is said and done, Brad has done a fine job of bringing Project Apex to a successful conclusion. Through his experiences, he has learned a tremendous amount about project management. He has learned that a well-documented and well-designed project management process is essential if his organization is to continue to benefit from the projects they pursue.

Brad has learned many valuable lessons about the benefits of planning.

And he has learned that projects are really small investments that his organization makes, making projects sort of like a business enterprise—something he had never fully appreciated as a technical contributor. He has come to appreciate the role that management plays, and how important their support is to project success.

He's found out that risk and uncertainty aren't quite so intimidating, as long as you have a process for dealing with them. In fact, he's learned that nearly everything he did related to project management was supported by a sound process—including communication and documentation!

He has learned that life as a project manager is all about getting things done through others—a radical departure from his previous job duties. Brad has learned that being a project manager is a surprisingly demanding job, but a job that has been extremely rewarding for him, nonetheless.

"I'd really like to try doing this again," Brad says to himself, just as his phone starts ringing. He picks it up before the second ring. It's his boss, Susan.

"Brad, I'd like you to stop by my office right after lunch today" says the voice on the other end of the line.

Brad smiles as he unwraps his turkey sandwich. This time he knows what to expect.

Project Manager's Checklist for Chapter 12

❑ Early termination of a project—as long as it's done for the right business reasons—should be viewed as a success, not a failure.

❑ Several unique issues and challenges are likely to surface at the end of projects. Some you can anticipate and plan for—many you cannot.

❑ Treat the last few activities that have to get done as a separate, small project. Plan and schedule them, then aggressively drive them to completion. Failure to complete the project in a timely fashion can significantly impact the customer's perception of satisfaction and success.

❑ Transfer everything you've learned to others within your organization who may benefit from your experiences—good or bad.

❑ Good Luck in your future project management endeavors!

Index